A Miller's Tale

By
ALAN MILLER

Edited by
Mark Hooper

ISBN No. 0 9527932 1 0

Published by
Middlesbrough Football and Athletic Club (1986) Ltd, 1996.

Designed and Printed by Hillprint Ltd, Bishop Auckland.

Front Cover Picture by Robert Wilson,
reproduced from his book, "One".

INTRODUCTION

When Alan Miller started his diary, he could hardly of imagined the drama that would follow. It was a season of ups and downs, both personal and footballing, as Middlesbrough Football Club enjoyed a rollercoaster first season in the Premier League.

Alan tells his personal tale of the season. From the high of starting the season as the club's number one to the low of life on the fringes. There is also the life away from football that is rarely brought into the spotlight - personal tragedies that bring footballing dilemmas into perspective and the pressures that come with celebrity status.

The diary is also the story of a year in the life of Middlesbrough Football Club. It is an incredible year that starts with the move to the awesome Cellnet Riverside Stadium. There are the extraordinary signings which took the football world by storm including the move that brought the Samba beat to Teesside with the signing of the Brazilian Juninho. On the pitch, it is a season which starts with Boro mixing with the league leaders and follows with a disastrous run of results that leaves both fans and players demoralised.

But more than that, the tale gives an insight into what it is like to live the schoolboy's dream and become a professional footballer. As only a player could, the book gives a rare look behind the scenes at a Premier League club - into the dressing rooms and training grounds, on foreign trips and on the pitch. It reveals the conflicts and individual set-backs as well as the moments of humour and togetherness that a good team spirit breeds.

The book shows the precarious nature of life at a football club where an injury can cause havoc and a season can turn around in the blink of an eye. And as the final twist in this tale reveals, how a footballer's life can change in the space of a few minutes.

Mark Hooper

Alan Miller was born in Essex in March 1970. As a young goalkeeper he started his career at Arsenal and graduated from the FA School of Excellence at Lilleshall. After several years in the shadows at Highbury as cover for David Seaman, Alan took the chance of regular first team football and joined Middlesbrough Football Club. After his £425,000 switch to Teesside, Alan helped the club win promotion to the Premier League. Throughout the 1995/96 season, Alan kept this diary. But first he introduces the management and players at Middlesbrough Football Club who feature on these pages.

INTRODUCING...

BRYAN ROBSON

The gaffer. He was the reason I came to Middlesbrough and it was the same for a lot of other players. I get on well with him and he earns a lot of respect. He's a different person as a manager to when he was a player. He doesn't shout so much and prefers not to have a go at the players. He's still quite young and learning like the players. Maybe he would have done a few things differently if he had the time again but I'm sure he will do well and become a great manager.

VIV ANDERSON

He's Bryan's sidekick, always bubbly and having a laugh. I remember when I was an apprentice at Arsenal, him and Charlie Nicholas were the only players you heard and he hasn't changed. If you've got a problem he says 'don't ask me, I'm a player' but if you ask something about the playing side he says "don't ask me, I'm management"! But he bridges the gap really well between the players and the manager and joins in the five-a-sides. You just have to make sure he doesn't score because you'll never hear the last of it.

JOHN PICKERING

The first team coach and an excellent one at that. He's the unsung hero of the club because he puts so much work in. He provided some continuity when Viv and Bryan came in. His training is quality and I rate him very highly.

MIKE KELLY

I've known Mike since I was 14 when I was at Lilleshall and he is a fantastic goalkeeping coach. I've been lucky to have worked with two of the best in him and Bob Wilson. He knows my character and despite the odd run-in I appreciate what he has done.

NEIL COX

My old mucker and probably the player I most go around with as we joined the club at the same time and live very close to each other. We've both got a similar sense of humour. He's always bubbly in the dressing room and has plenty to say. Also one of the best golfers at the club.

CURTIS FLEMING

Another great lad who lives near me in Yarm. He's a good player to have in your side and never gives up any lost causes. You know exactly what you're getting. He's very proud of being Irish but Viv always take the Mickey out of him saying he's English because he was born in Manchester. He had a baby daughter at the start of the 1996-7 season so he has a few bags under his eyes coming into training.

DEREK WHYTE

One of my singing partners when we have a night out with his version of Leroy Brown which is brilliant. He's a great lad to have in the dressing room as he's always laughing and has a great sense of humour. He has been known to be called "high hair" while he's been trying to grow his hair long. He has to put loads of wax on it to keep it under control and if you saw it with none on, you would understand the nickname. He keeps telling us it's in a transitional period.

STEVE VICKERS

Player of the year for the 95/96 season and deservedly so, playing just behind the two centre-backs. Although not as loud as some players in the dressing room, Steve has a very dry sense of humour and is very quick-witted. If you are wearing any dodgy gear in training, Steve is the first one to let you know.

NIGEL PEARSON

Otherwise known as "the pest"! He's always mucking around and taking the Mickey, even when you're trying to relax and just have a quiet time. He was responsible for all the graffiti and drawings on the walls at Ayresome Park which were brilliant and are featured throughout this diary. He is great for dressing room atmosphere and an excellent captain. He's the type of person who would super-glue your shoes to the floor! Mind you, I shouldn't have said that as it might give him ideas. He's also my room partner.

NICK BARMBY

'Barms' was our first big signing. He is another player with a very dry sense of humour and not frightened to use it. He was normally the last to finish training as he stayed behind to do extra. It was a shame to see him leave to go to Everton in November 1996 after such a short time at Boro but he is a quality player with a big international future.

ROBBIE MUSTOE

"Snouty" as Mike Kelly calls him. Robbie's a really well liked player who takes a lot of stick really well and gives it back. Sometimes the more stick you get the more popular you are and Robbie has got a brilliant personality. He has proved that he's an important part of the team and a lot of people have taken notice. He's always immaculate in everything he does.

JUNINHO

The Frankie Dettori lookalike! Signed in October 1995 and since then his English has come on leaps and bounds and he seems to be really happy on Teesside. He played for the Brazilian Olympic side in the summer of 1996 and keeps getting better. He's another who likes to take the Mickey if you're wearing any dodgy clothes, although I think he needs to look a little closer to home with some of the gear he puts on!

ALAN MOORE

Alan is known as "lively" simply because of the fact that he will do as little work as humanly possible. He doesn't even go out for a warm-up before games. He's another with a very dry personality. He might be seen to be quiet but I think this is very deceptive. He has been very unlucky not to play more because of the formation we played.

GARY WALSH

The keeper signed at the start of the 95/96 season and my rival for the number one shirt. Dubbed Mike Flowers after the singer who did Wonderwall. He's a Lancashire lad who's a big Rugby League fan. Although we were both vying for the number one spot in the team, there was never any animosity except when Essex played Lancashire in one of the cricket cup finals. He got one over on me that day when we were beaten easily.

PHIL WHELAN

Some of the fans got on Phil's back when he first joined Boro but he showed great character and won them over with some good performances. I went on holiday with Phil in the summer after this diary finished and had a great laugh. He's another one who's very quick to take the Mickey and it's quite rare that you get one over on him. For some reason, the kit never seems to fit him properly - I don't know why! The heaviest player in the club.

CLAYTON BLACKMORE

Blacky is another player who's had a frustrating time. He played a lot in the promotion season but since then his chances have been limited. He's got a great first touch and one hell of a strike and is still a good player. He's also a very good golfer. He could talk for England - or should I say Wales.

JAMIE POLLOCK

Jamie left at the end of the 95/96 season to go to Spain and since then has returned to England with Bolton. He's a local lad and took a lot of stick about his weight from the lads. He will never change his shape but he's got a good engine on him anyway

PHIL STAMP

Following Jamie's departure, Stampy is the only local lad in the first team. He's big and strong and full of running. It's hard to believe how young he is and has a great future in front of him. He's a lovely, genuine lad who often comes out with funny sayings. He knows a lot of people and if you ever want anything he's the man to ask.

CRAIG HIGNETT

Higgy is another player who has been forced out of the first team action. He's a very quick-witted Scouser who always has plenty to say for himself and is good value in the dressing room. In the first half of the 95/96 season he was probably our best player so it must have been very frustrating for him to lose his place.

JAN FJORTOFT

Jan was frozen out by the arrival of Fabrizio Ravanelli at the start of the 96/97 season but he was, at one stage, our record transfer. He fits in well and speaks brilliant English. He's also a great finisher who seems to score goals out of nothing.

A Miller's Tale

BEN ROBERTS

Ben's a great young goalkeeper who hasn't played in the first team yet but he has gained some valuable experience with loan spells at various clubs. He's a great lad to get on with and has a fantastic future. But he's another one who plays off a suspect golf handicap.

CHRIS MORRIS

He's been a great servant to the club and still has a lot to offer as a player. It looks like he might get a free transfer at the end of the season. He's a very easy person to get on with and will do a great job for someone if and when he does go.

JOHN HENDRIE

"Happy" was probably Boro's best signing over the last 10 years and it was a sad day when he went to Barnsley in October 1996. He was always a livewire in the dressing room and had some of the funniest dance routines I've ever seen. He always had an uncanny knack of getting the words wrong when singing any type of song - his favourite was Stand and Deliver by Adam Ant. He'll be very popular at Barnsley, I'm sure.

GRAHAM KAVANAGH

Kav left Boro to join Stoke early in the 96/97 season. I think he'll be back in the top flight because he's a good player but the move was right for him. He got on well with Curtis Fleming and Alan Moore because of the Irish connection and was a nice lad to get on with.

JAIME MORENO

Jaime was a skilful player but never really had the consistency to make it at Boro and he left to go to the US in the summer of 1996. He picked up English very well and soon worked out the English sense of humour and joined in with the best of them. He changed quite a lot and was good fun.

PAUL WILKINSON

Wilko or 'Trigger' as he's sometimes known. He's a lovely lad who I've got a lot of time for. He always takes everything very slowly. He did a good job at Boro but was on the fringes for a while before leaving for Barnsley.

BRANCO

He was very funny, making funny faces behind people's backs. He was an experienced player - we never quite found out how old he was! The only thing I could have a go at him for is the comments he made criticising John Pickering and Viv which were out of order. The headline in the Sun was good though - "Branco - Viv's a Planko". It soon appeared on the treatment room door and everyone had a good laugh about it, calling Viv "Planko".

EMERSON

He's got a great bubbly personality and is always smiling and singing although the songs are normally in Brazilian. He has picked up English quickly. He is big and strong and was a great signing, becoming an instant hit with the fans. He's had a few problems settling in up on Teesside but he should get over them.

MIKKEL BECK

I haven't really known Mikkel that long but he's another who's settled in well in really difficult circumstances when he arrived. He couldn't play for ages because of a dispute with his former club in Germany but he showed remarkable patience during that time, training hard and never getting dejected. He was desperate to get involved which was a good sign and made a good impression when he broke into the side.

A Miller's Tale

FABRIZIO RAVANELLI

He was an incredible signing for us having just won the European Cup with Juventus. You could tell how much their fans thought of him when Boro played Juve in a friendly in Italy. He settled in well considering he couldn't speak much English and got off to a flying start. Let's hope he continues to pull that shirt over his head. I think he found it difficult when things weren't going so well as he's used to winning things. He's definitely got an aura about him and everything he does has a touch of class about it.

Happy days! The lads celebrate back at Ayresome Park on the morning after winning promotion from the First Division. Not much training done on that day!

A Miller's Tale

THURSDAY 6 JULY 1995

First day back at Ayresome Park after an enjoyable summer break. Most of the other players are due back next week. The few exceptions today were the heavyweights of the team - myself, Jamie Pollock, Phil Whelan and Neil Cox - need I say more?

I didn't see the other lads until 2.00pm because of the problems I've had with my shoulder. Bob Ward, the club physio, wanted to go through some exercises to strengthen the damaged area. During the end of last season's First Division-winning campaign I had a lot of problems with my shoulder and in the close season I had a camera put in. They found a slight tear in the tendon. I could have had an operation but I would have missed the beginning of the season and I decided to try and play on with it. I just hope I don't live to regret it in the long term. Sometimes you just have to carry on through injuries.

The first player I saw today was Neil Cox who, after giving me one of his infamous grins, told me about his exploits during the summer. After seeing Coxy I then saw Phil Whelan in the shower (not a pretty sight). On observation, he looked surprisingly fit and well, as did Jamie Pollock, although I found out afterwards he's been running for the past three weeks. It looks as though I may have come back the heaviest, so after seeing Bob, I had a jog around the pitch.

It's hard to believe this was the same place where only two months earlier there were so many ecstatic and emotional scenes after the Luton game, which eventually won us promotion. After being away for a while and with no crowd, it brought home how run-down the ground has become. Last time I left the buzz of excitement was overwhelming. Today, it was an eerie, quiet place with no-one there.

Now we can look forward to playing in the Cellnet Riverside Stadium. It is great for me to be going back into the Premier League at the first attempt and, with the new stadium on the way, it is vital we

A Miller's Tale

are in the top flight. It wouldn't be the same if we were looking forward to going to the new ground still in the First Division.

I finished off the day with the first of what I'm sure will be many games of golf this season with Coxy, Bob Ward and Robbie Mustoe.

FRIDAY 7 JULY 1995

The first thing that greeted me this morning was Jamie Pollock's new skinhead haircut (or is that scare cut?). I think he could be in for some severe stick when all the other players are back.

We trained this morning at Kirklevington prison near Yarm and went back to Ayresome Park for an afternoon session.

To our surprise, when we got into the gymnasium we realised why first team coach John Pickering had had a smug grin on his face all morning. There to greet us was an aerobics teacher. You could see after a couple of minutes who were the dancers of the team and who were definitely not, but I won't mention any names (Mr Whelan!).

After the initial Mickey-taking, the session was actually quite good with all of us getting a really good sweat on.

Before I left, Phil and I weighed ourselves.

       Alan Miller: 15st 2lb
       Phil Whelan: 14st 13lb

Afterwards, Phil challenged me to a £10 bet that by next Thursday (weigh day) I won't be lighter than him. Although I've got to make up 3lb, he told me he's going to Blackpool at the weekend with a few mates, so I consider this a fair bet. Watch out Blackpool!

MONDAY 10 JULY 1995

After a weekend off, we were back training this afternoon at Kirklevington.

Only 2lb behind Phil Whelan when weighed afterwards. Getting closer!
Alan Miller: 15st 0lb
Phil Whelan: 14st 12lb

My old team Arsenal have signed David Platt for £4.75 million - another good buy for them, I think. The media says he nearly signed for us - another player that has slipped through the net? We've been linked with a lot of players like Kanchelskis, Platt and John Collins but we still haven't signed a new player yet. I'm sure the gaffer, Bryan Robson, has got quite a few players in mind and he's got the money to spend, but getting them seems to be a bit more difficult than he probably imagined. It's a little worrying.

Neil Cox, Jamie Pollock, Curtis Fleming, Robbie Mustoe, John Hendrie and I attended the launch of a new lager for the Premier League (Carlsberg Premier) at the Dickens Inn pub in Middlesbrough.

TUESDAY 11 JULY 1995

Trained this morning then back to Ayresome Park for another session of aerobics - I think we're slowly getting the hang of it!

Robbie Mustoe, Phil Whelan, Jamie Pollock, the kit man Tommy Johnson and I went to see how the new stadium was coming along. We had a guided tour of the site with Keith Lamb, the club's chief executive. The stadium looked absolutely fantastic and is going to be one of the best in the country. Having said that, there is still a

A Miller's Tale

lot of work to be done and there is only six weeks to do it in. It's going to be touch and go.

Apparently, the total cost of the stadium will eventually be £22 million. Chief Executive Keith Lamb was saying that we have sold 14,000 season tickets so far and when we buy a couple of players between now and the start of the season it will go up to 20,000. When quizzed about who the players would be he said: "I can't tell you yet, but they definitely won't be defenders."

The total cost of the stadium will eventually be £22M.

After training today the last unofficial weigh-in took place between Phil Whelan and myself. The result was as follows:

Alan Miller:	14st 13lb
Phil Whelan:	14st 12lb

Only 1lb in it. Official weigh-in on Thursday.

WEDNESDAY 12 JULY 1995

Reports in the papers say that Andrei Kanchelskis wants to come to Middlesbrough and team up with Bryan Robson. He would cost £6 million. It's a lot of money but he would be a great player for us.

Played golf with Neil Cox. We met the comedian Roy 'Chubby' Brown on the golf course, who is a fanatical Boro supporter. He said if ever we were in Blackpool, just to turn up at one of his shows and he would get us in, no problem. Halfway down the 11th, he shouted back towards the clubhouse: "Mind you, if you sign for Sunderland you can f*** off!"

Some of the members nearly choked on their gin and tonics.

THURSDAY 13 JULY 1995

Lost my bet with Phil Whelan. Final weight:

Alan Miller: 15st 0lb
Phil Whelan: 14st 12lb

After being measured, I had actually grown a ¼ in to 6ft 3½in and argued that the bet should be null and void due to a technicality. Unfortunately, Phil wasn't having it and I had to hand over a tenner. I wouldn't mind, but Phil and Jamie went to Redcar races last night and they got a tip for a horse in the last race at 20-1. The horse duly romped home and Phil won £800. Cheers Phil, I didn't want to go anyway!

Everybody was back today. The manager looks quite heavy and has obviously had a good summer. But he is still up at the front in the running with assistant manager Viv Anderson languishing somewhere at the rear, as usual!

FRIDAY 14 JULY 1995

Former Boro striker Uwe Fuchs has signed for Millwall for £325,000. I'm pleased he has found a club in England, which he really wanted, although it's not in the Premier League where he would rather have played.

He did such a good job for Middlesbrough when he came here on loan last season and scored goals when we were struggling a bit. Everyone was surprised when the manager let him go, but he must have had his reasons.

Uwe was a cult hero here but he didn't fit into the gaffer's plans. I remember the night the manager told him, he was devastated and

A Miller's Tale

I felt really sorry for him. He loved it here and was desperate to stay. I think all of us would wish him well - but maybe not if we draw Millwall in one of the cups.

SATURDAY/SUNDAY 15 & 16 JULY 1995

Spent the weekend at Nigel Pearson's house with his wife, Nicky, kids and my girlfriend Joanne. We both felt absolutely knackered after this week's training but had a good weekend.

MONDAY 17 JULY 1995

Morning and afternoon sessions today, and both sessions were very hard with temperatures in the 80's. Quite a few of the lads were showing a few signs of fatigue, mentioning no names!

Jamie Pollock pulled out of training with shin problems. Bob Ward said he hopes it's not the start of a stress fracture. John Hendrie also pulled out with knee problems and had a precautionary scan. Hopefully it's just the hard ground - or is it his age? Only joking, Happy!

TUESDAY 18 JULY 1995

Nick Barmby has refused a new contract at Spurs and supposedly pulled out of buying a new house down south. So, inevitably, his name has been linked with a move to Boro, especially as he is from the north and his wife apparently wants to move back.

We must have been linked with more players than anyone this summer, yet still no-one new has arrived. It can only be a matter of time surely.

WEDNESDAY 19 JULY 1995

£6.5 million - that's the figure Spurs want for Barmby according to the press. It's absolutely ridiculous. A year ago you could have bought him for around £2 million. I don't think the manager will entertain that valuation and I don't blame him. The whole transfer situation has gone mad!!

Some of the money the clubs are paying is barmy. As a player it's out of your hands, you can't influence what happens in the transfer market, but you wonder where it is going to end. It puts a lot of pressure on the players because they have to perform straight away.

THURSDAY 20 JULY 1995

Manchester United have accepted our bid of £5 million for Andrei Kanchelskis, but Everton have matched the offer. Apparently, he will have talks with both clubs over the weekend so we're keeping our fingers crossed!

Coxy and I played golf against Bob Ward and Mike Kelly - the club's goalkeeping coach. We won the first nine holes, but they won the last and the match was halved. Mike keeps moaning that my handicap is too high, I think it was just because he didn't play very well. Chin up, Mike!

FRIDAY 21 JULY 1995

Andrei Kanchelskis has signed for Everton. It's a massive blow for Bryan Robson and all of us at Middlesbrough. Nothing seems to be going right for the gaffer in the transfer market. He still seems quite calm about the situation, but surely deep down even he must be a little concerned. If only we could sign a big name soon, it would be a massive boost for everyone at the club and on Teesside. The gaffer told the press he's still after quite a few big name players. We need a big squad to go into the Premier League and the players know we have to have competition for places to do well.

SATURDAY 22 JULY 1995

We played a practice game today at Ayresome Park amongst ourselves, the first of the season. Considering it was the first game, the quality was very good until late in the second half when everybody became very tired. One of the teams tried a new system which worked very well. The system we played is more commonly known as the Christmas tree formation and lines up as follows:

```
                o                    Forwards
           o         o               Midfield/forwards
        o       o        o           Midfield
     o       o       o       o       Defenders
```

The gaffer explained it in detail with John Pickering and Viv Anderson afterwards. He told us all that during the coming season we will have to get used to playing various systems and formations to give opposition teams different problems when they play against us. Most of the players agree that the system will benefit us.

The final score of the match was 0-0. First clean sheet of the season. Many more to come, I hope.

After a hard week's training, I decided to have a night out with Coxy and Paul Wilkinson. It's funny because when I was at Arsenal everybody lived quite far apart and we rarely got together away from training. When I moved up here it was completely different. I joined around the same time as Neil Cox and Clayton Blackmore. Me and Coxy lived in digs together so we built up a good relationship. You always tend to mix in those circles and socialise together.

MONDAY 24 JULY 1995

Alan Smith, a very good friend of mine in my days at Arsenal, announced today he is retiring from football due to a knee injury. This is really sad news. I knew he was having a lot of problems with his knee but had no idea it was career threatening.

Arsenal announced they will hold a benefit game for "Smudge" which is the least he deserves after being such a great servant for my old club.

Although it is always devastating for a player to have to retire early, I suppose, in retrospect, Smudge has had a fairly long and very successful career with Leicester and, of course, Arsenal. In that time he has won two Championship medals, a Cup Winners' Cup medal, an FA Cup winners' medal and two League Cup winners' medals as well as two Golden Boots for being top scorer in the top flight.

I know that, at 32, he could have had at least another three years at the highest level, but he has finished at the very top of his profession and will be remembered as a top class striker.

He's a very sensible and intelligent person, and it wouldn't surprise me if he pursues a career in the world of TV and media coverage of sport. He's a bit like Gary Lineker, a model professional. I had some great times with Smudge at Arsenal rooming with him over the years. People think he's very quiet but he's actually got a great, dry sense of humour.

He always kept himself out of trouble. He used to be really proud that he had never been booked and the players had a go at him saying: "How can you be a centre-forward and not get booked?" Then, in the cup final, he picked up his first ever booking. In one way he was annoyed but he was also quite pleased because the lads couldn't give him any more stick.

If he becomes as successful outside of football as he has been in it, he'll go a hell of a long way. Good luck Smudger!

TUESDAY 25 JULY 1995

We played our first friendly game this evening against Hartlepool. We won the game 1-0 but we weren't really at full strength as the manager mixed the team around so we could accommodate two games in three days - the next being Darlington on Thursday. It wasn't a great performance by any means, but considering it was our first game, it wasn't bad at all. We experimented with the Christmas tree formation again and it had a mixed reaction - some liked it, some didn't. I believe it's something well worth trying. Craig Hignett scored the winning goal from the penalty spot. Another clean sheet, I suppose.

FRIDAY 28 JULY 1995

From here to eternity, that's what it feels like after travelling 7½ hours to get from Teesside to Sweden for our pre-season tour. On arrival at Oslo airport, Tommy Johnson, the kit man, began to tell all the lads about his trials and tribulations here during the war and what a lovely country Sweden was. No-one had the heart to tell him we were in Norway. How we won the war, I'll never know! Don't panic, Mr Mainwaring.

After arriving in Oslo, it was another two hours on a coach over the border to where we are staying in Sweden and all the lads became very tired and restless. Quite a few comments were shouted down to the front of the bus, demanding to know who had organised the trip.

Just when we thought we'd seen it all, we pulled up outside what looked like a Little Chef. We then realised this is where we are staying, but not in the motel, out around the back in chalets for two. It's like something out of "Escape to Victory".

After putting our bags in our rooms we went for something to eat which seemed to consist of Ryvitas and beetroot. Lovely!!

I'm rooming with Nigel Pearson and, after choosing our bunk beds, we try and get some sleep. It's now 1.15am.

SATURDAY 29 JULY 1995

I wish I had a camera with me to take some pictures of the lads in their chalets. They would be very amusing pictures.

We played our first game of the tour tonight and beat Saffle SF 4-1. It was a fairly easy game but the lads worked hard and we should have really won by a lot more. After the game we had a meal with another lot of beetroot. They must have a beetroot mountain in Sweden which they're trying to get rid of. Still no sign of life anywhere near where we are staying. They're not silly these managers, are they?

SUNDAY 30 JULY 1995

Played a team called Vastvarmland and beat them 5-0. It was a very easy game which we should have won even more easily. The gaffer gave all of us a bollocking afterwards and said we have to be more professional this season, starting from now, and we are all playing for our places.

There was nothing to do in the evening so we decided to make a small camp fire and all sat outside the chalets with a few beers and some music, with some help from guest singers Derek Whyte (Leroy Brown) and Chris Morris (Barnacle Bill the Sailor). It wasn't the first, and definitely won't be the last, time we hear these songs during the coming season. With a few jokes and Mickey-taking, it didn't turn out to be a bad night.

MONDAY 31 JULY 1995

We went over some defensive tactics this morning for the way we are going to play during the season. After his outburst last night, the gaffer was in a good mood and seemed quite relaxed. After training we were taken to a small beach area by a lake for a spot of swimming, volleyball and - for Bob Ward, Neil Cox and myself - water skiing.

TUESDAY 1 AUGUST 1995

We drew 2-2 with Norwegian side Kongsvinger. We played very well tonight with a lot of positive things coming out of the game but it was followed by another boring night back at the barracks.

WEDNESDAY 2 AUGUST 1995

It was our last game and we beat Ham-Kam of Norway 1-0 with the gaffer scoring the winning goal. Viv Anderson played at the back because of a few injuries and he played very well. It's hard to believe he's now 39.

It was also our last night of the tour, and, after the game, we travelled to Oslo. After checking into a hotel, we went on a night out which Jan Fjortoft had organised for us at a night-club. Jan has been under unbelievable pressure because, on arriving in Norway, he said this would be the week of our dreams and it's turned out to be a nightmare.

This time we did have a good night and met a few of the Liverpool players at the club. They had just been beaten 3-0 by the Norwegian national team. They didn't seem too bothered about it.

Why is it that whenever you go out and have a good drink, you always end up stuffing your face full of greasy hamburgers in the early hours of the morning? Well, I think it was a hamburger! At least it wasn't beetroot.

THURSDAY 3 AUGUST 1995

Early start this morning for the return flight to Newcastle. There were a lot of tired looking people at breakfast this morning. It's amazing what happens when you're threatened with a two week's wages fine for being late - everybody was down on time.

The lads couldn't wait to get home. Having said that, it was a good trip in terms of team spirit. It has been great throughout all the highs and lows of the past week. As soon as I got in, I said hello to my girlfriend Jo and then crashed out for a couple of hours. She must have been well impressed with that.

FRIDAY 4 AUGUST 1995

The gaffer has made a bid of £5.25 million for Nick Barmby, but it was later rejected by Alan Sugar, Spurs' chairman. I can't see anybody paying more than that for him. The gaffer told Spurs that was his final offer.

After training we had our photographs taken in the new strip, home and away. These are always so chaotic and this was no exception, taking over an hour. The funniest part was when the gaffer asked where the Championship trophy was. Someone had forgotten to bring it down for the team photograph. We couldn't believe it. Surely that was the most important thing to be on it. We had all worked so hard to get it and we wanted to show it off!

After this, we had to go to Newcastle to record a song for the new stadium. We didn't mind because we were apparently on 20 per cent of the profits, but as Phil Whelan pointed out, 20 per cent of nothing doesn't work out to a lot! Ben Roberts was a bit upset when they asked him politely if he wouldn't mind standing away from the microphone.

SATURDAY 5 AUGUST 1995

Day off today but it was announced on the 10.00pm news that we've signed Nick Barmby from Spurs for £5.25 million. At last we've made a signing and a big one at that, even though I think it's far too much money. Having said that, he's only 21 and may, at some later stage, be sold for a big fee again, so maybe this is also a big investment for the club.

This will be a massive boost for all of us. I can't wait to see the lads' reaction tomorrow at training. Maybe he will come with us on our tour to Scotland next week. It may also set the ball rolling concerning other signings. We have been linked with Celtic's John Collins and the Brazilian, Juninho.

SUNDAY 6 AUGUST 1995

We found out this morning that we had to take our training kit in our own bags to Scotland. This was unbelievable. We are now supposed to be a Premier League club but we still have to take our own kit. I wouldn't mind but we were travelling by coach to Scotland and it would have only taken one skip to put all the kit in and just simply put in on to the coach and take it off when we got there.

After complaining to skipper Nigel Pearson, he in turn had a moan at our kit man, Tommy Johnson. Unfortunately, Tom didn't take this harassment very well and nearly handed his notice in. In the end, we all took our own kit, just to get off Tommy's back.

Shortly afterwards, I asked Tommy for my gloves which I had asked him to look after at the end of the last game in Norway. Needless to say, he couldn't find them but, just before I was going to go mad, I realised if I started on him he might crack up and walk out on the club for good. I think having Nigel Pearson on your case is enough for anybody in one day!

After a 3½ hour coach journey, we arrived at Stirling in Scotland where we are staying. After last week's trip, the hotel seems like the Ritz - we're not used to towels in the rooms. To pass time on the coach journey, I played a bit of Chas & Dave which was good for a giggle. Nigel Pearson is always taking the Mickey out of my London accent so he loved it. He became a Cockney for 20 minutes! Mind you, when I played a bit of Englebert Humperdink I think I pushed the boat out a little bit too far.

MONDAY 7 AUGUST 1995

We drew with St Johnstone 2-2 tonight and considering we have quite a few injuries at the moment - Jan Fjortoft, Curtis Fleming, Nigel Pearson, Alan Moore and John Hendrie - we played well and really should have won the game. Overall, it was quite positive with Jamie Pollock playing his first game of the pre-season and doing well.

John Collins was at the game with his agent. After playing well again at the weekend, it would apparently take £3.5 million to £4 million now for Celtic to part company with him. It was only £2.5 million last month. I wonder if it's got anything to do with us paying £5.25 million for Nick Barmby!

TUESDAY 8 AUGUST 1995

There was speculation in the papers this morning that the gaffer is trying to sign Gary Walsh from Manchester United. The fee would be around £750,000. I know he feels he needs another keeper at the club since the departure of Stephen Pears but I wouldn't have thought Gary Walsh would want to leave United and be a number two at any other club, so it would become a battle for the number one jersey. The gaffer wants this in every position in the team, no-one has the divine right for a place, and I suppose it's up to all of us to fight for them. It can only be good for the side. We will have to see what happens.

I think it's inevitable that the gaffer will bring another keeper to the club at some stage, although I happen to think Ben Roberts is, and will become, a very good keeper. It's a shame he hasn't been on loan and gained some league experience. Maybe he will this season.

It would be easier for me if no-one came in - you'd rather have everything your own way - but life's not like that, especially not in football. I've just got to make sure I don't give whoever comes in a chance to take my place.

WEDNESDAY 9 AUGUST 1995

It seems as though we have been away on tour for a month or so after last week and this week's trip. I think everybody will be pleased to get back home on Saturday and back to some normality.

Nick Barmby trained with us for the first time today and looked very sharp. Some of the lads went to watch Rangers play in the first round of the European Cup. They only managed to beat the Cypriot Champions (whose name I can't even remember) 1-0. I'm glad I didn't go and watch it, besides I would have missed Michael Parkinson interviewing Tommy Cooper tonight. Nothing like watching Tommy to cheer you up. Egg bag, bag egg!

THURSDAY 10 AUGUST 1995

We drew with Hibs 0-0 tonight with Nick Barmby making his debut. He looked sharp and made some very good runs off the ball.

I saw Jim Leighton after the game and had a good chat with him. He was on loan at Arsenal for a while when I was injured with my slipped disc. I'm pleased for him because he's now back in the Scotland squad after having a very good season with Hibs. He's a perfect example of keeping your chin up and working hard to turn it your way when things are going against you, as they did for him in his last year at Manchester United. He's also a very nice bloke.

FRIDAY 11 AUGUST 1995

Gary Walsh today signed for Boro for £250,000. The gaffer said it's up to us all - Gary, Ben and myself - to fight for the number one shirt. Whoever plays well will keep his place.

My biggest hope is that I can start the season, not just because it's at Arsenal, but because I worked so hard all last year to become number one and to get back into the Premier League. I feel I've done nothing to warrant being left out for the first game. If, after the first few games, things haven't gone so well for me then, fair enough, but I think I've genuinely earned the right to play from the start and then for each of us to be judged on our merits. But you know what they say - it's a funny old game.

SATURDAY 12 AUGUST 1995

We beat Motherwell 4-1 today, with Craig Hignett scoring a hat-trick. He has now scored nine goals in our pre-season games. I'm really pleased for him because, at the end of last season, he nearly left the club on a free transfer, but he took a pay cut and decided to fight for his place. There's only one way to prove a point and that's on the pitch. He's certainly done that and has got a great chance of playing at Arsenal next weekend.

I gave a penalty away for Motherwell's goal, which I wasn't pleased with, but overall it was another good performance, and we are unbeaten this pre-season. I'm not sure if that's a good thing or not!

MONDAY 14 AUGUST 1995

I met Gary Walsh today and he seems a nice bloke. We trained morning and afternoon with Mike Kelly. I think Gary was surprised how hard we worked, especially as it was red hot. I should imagine he will sleep well tonight.

WEDNESDAY 16 AUGUST 1995

The squad numbers were announced and I was really happy to be given the number one jersey. It looks as if I will be playing on Sunday and now it's up to me to keep my place.

Squad numbers are as follows:
1. Alan Miller 2. Neil Cox 3. Chris Morris 4. Steve Vickers 5. Nigel Pearson 6. Derek Whyte 7. Nick Barmby 8. Jamie Pollock 9. Jan Fjortoft 10. John Hendrie 11. Robbie Mustoe 12. Alan Moore 13. Gary Walsh 14. Curtis Fleming 15. Phil Whelan 16. Bryan Robson 17. Clayton Blackmore 18. Graham Kavanagh 19. Jaime Moreno

20. Philip Stamp 21. Craig Hignett 22. Craig Liddle.

Interesting that the gaffer has given his beloved number 7 shirt to Nick Barmby.

FRIDAY 18 AUGUST 1995

We worked on defensive set pieces after our day off yesterday. It seemed to take quite a while for us to get organised. I suppose it's going to be a case of "It'll be alright on the night" - or day in this case.

SATURDAY 19 AUGUST 1995

We put the finishing touches to our preparation for tomorrow's game in training today and everybody is looking forward to it. It's strange to have the opening day of the season and not be involved.

Manchester United lost 3-1 at Aston Villa. I think Alex Ferguson will come under a lot of pressure if he doesn't sign some new faces soon.

I'm looking forward to tomorrow's game at Arsenal, a little nervous, but I think that's all part of it. I'm going to enjoy the game as much as possible. Playing in big matches in front of a packed house is what it's all about.

We're flying down in the morning. Flying is a great way to travel and leaves all the lads a lot fresher for the games instead of having a 4½ hour coach journey.

Arsenal 1 Middlesbrough 1 - what a great opening result for us and we even went 1-0 up. Nick Barmby scored on his debut after a great flick from Jan Fjortoft. Arsenal got one back about five minutes after us, which was quite close to half-time. It was a shame because it would have been very interesting if we could have gone in at half-time winning 1-0. After starting the game well, we fell away a bit in the second and we were under pressure for most of it, but we held out for a very well earned point.

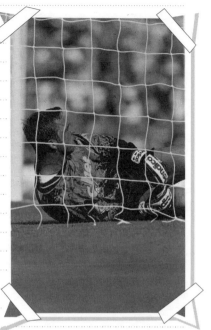

I got a great reception from the Arsenal fans, especially when I ran down to the North Bank. It was a great feeling. It was also enjoyable because I managed to play well, which is always nice when returning to your old club.

In the back of the net for the game against my old team at Highbury. Unfortunately, I had to pick the ball out once though we got a good draw.

I think all the Middlesbrough fans there had a great day. They certainly made a lot of noise. They're going to be very important to us this year.

Went out for a drink after the game with Neil Cox who stayed down in London with me and some friends.

MONDAY 21 AUGUST 1995

We had a day off after the game so I went shopping and met Uwe Fuchs for lunch in London. It was good to see him again. Gave him a poster of Winston Churchill to hang in his new apartment to make him feel at home!

TUESDAY 22 AUGUST 1995

Reports on the news said there are problems with a licence to hold the game at the new stadium on Saturday because of access to the ground. Earlier, the game was announced as a 30,000 sell-out so the fans will be absolutely gutted if it doesn't go ahead. We're supposed to be training there tomorrow.

WEDNESDAY 23 AUGUST 1995

The whole team went to the new Cellnet Riverside Stadium to have a look around. It looks absolutely magnificent, but there are quite a lot of things to be completed and it looks 50/50 if the game will go ahead. There are apparently 12 different targets to reach by noon on Friday before the club can be issued with a safety certificate. We all desperately want the game to go ahead.

The new stadium is going to be a world apart from Ayresome Park. I remember the first time I ever played there was with Arsenal just after the Coca-Cola Cup final in 1993. We flew up and it was the worst, windiest, wettest day ever. My first impressions certainly weren't very good. We lost 1-0, George Graham went mad afterwards and we were just desperate to get out of there. I remember sitting on the bench thinking that I didn't fancy playing there very much. It's funny that I ended up signing for Boro. I did get a chance to see the ground in a better light beforehand though.

When I joined, everybody knew we were moving. Ayresome Park was a bit neglected and everything had fallen into disrepair. It was sad to see a famous old ground get into such a state, but the place always created an unbelievable atmosphere. Teams never liked coming to play us.

You can tell how much the ground meant to people. Looking back to the last game last season, the farewell game, the atmosphere was electric. I will never forget walking around the pitch at the end. We had won promotion but I think the fact that it was the last game was more important to the fans, it was a very emotional day.

FRIDAY 25 AUGUST 1995

The game is definitely going ahead tomorrow and everybody is delighted. It's going to be a hard one. Chelsea have yet to concede a goal in two games.

SATURDAY 26 AUGUST 1995

We arrived at the Cellnet Riverside Stadium early (11.45am) for a pre-match meal in the new restaurant, only to find that the sprinklers had gone off in the kitchens ruining all the food. Not only did we have no food, but all the executive lounges also had nothing except sandwiches. We had to go to the Norton Hall hotel to get lunch and then come back which was hardly great preparation.

Despite the teething problems, we beat Chelsea 2-0, a great result with goals from Craig Hignett and Jan Fjortoft. It was an amazing occasion in the new stadium and the atmosphere was electric.

It's incredible to think we are now playing in front of full houses in a fantastic new stadium. It must have been a wonderful occasion for the fans and I'm just happy to have been part of it. Whatever happens from now onwards, whenever anyone looks back at the team sheet for the first game at the Riverside, they will see the name of Alan Miller there.

The club has been promised a lot over the years and the fans can now realise that the chairman means what he says. This club is really going places.

It was important to get off to a winning start at the new ground. I think if we can carry on the way we are playing and keeping it tight at the back, we might surprise a few people this season. Early days yet though.

SUNDAY 27 AUGUST 1995

Went to Redcar Races today with my family and girlfriend Jo. Neil Cox and Phil Whelan also went with their girlfriends and Mike Kelly and his family. We had a good day, but weren't very lucky with the horses. I backed one at 20-1 in the 1.00 and it didn't finish until 2.15! It was that late in it had to tiptoe back to the stables! Paul Daniels' horse won the last race, "That's Magic".

MONDAY 28 AUGUST 1995

Started preparing today for the derby with Newcastle on Wednesday. They won again yesterday, 2-0 against Sheffield Wednesday at Hillsborough, and have won all three games they've played. It's going to be a tough one for us but we're looking forward to it.

WEDNESDAY 30 AUGUST 1995

We trained this morning and everybody's in good spirits. We travelled up to Newcastle in the afternoon and had lunch at a hotel, followed by a very enjoyable sleep in the afternoon. When we arrived at St James' Park, it looked magnificent. They've done an amazing job with the stadium.

After the team talk, and shortly before the warm up, Roy 'Chubby' Brown came into the dressing room with a big red and white rosette on his chest. He started reeling off various jokes about Peter Beardsley and especially Michael Barrymore. I don't think I'd better repeat them. It probably did us a favour because it was quite a tense atmosphere before such a big game and he had us in stitches. It relaxed quite a few of us.

The atmosphere at the game was electric and we were under pressure right from the start, but, funnily enough, Jamie Pollock had the best chance of the first half. David Ginola was tremendous and gave Neil Cox a very hard night. After the game, Coxy said he had knees like Paul McGrath from being twisted and turned so much.

We held out until the 67th minute when Ferdinand scored after a great cross from Ginola. They had quite a few good chances in the second half and we again defended very well. In fact, we should have come away with a point when Peacock blatantly fouled Jamie Pollock in the area in the last minute, but the referee didn't give it. I suppose he realised he probably would never get out of the ground if he had given it. So, even though we knew they had the majority of the game, we were still disappointed not to get a point. Our fans were fantastic all night and even after the final whistle.

THURSDAY 31 AUGUST 1995

I picked up a groin strain during last night's game and it was very sore this morning so I had to have treatment.

The other lads relaxed at Springs Health Club on Teesside Park with some swimming and massages. We went out in the evening to celebrate the birth of Robbie Mustoe's little baby boy, Elliott. We ended up at a club in Middlesbrough called The Theatre and, on Thursday, it's 70's night which is absolutely brilliant. The DJ wears a big afro wig (Viv Anderson 1978) and rides about on a Chopper Bike.

FRIDAY 1 SEPTEMBER 1995

Treatment this morning and the injury was still a bit sore. Bob Ward has allowed me home for the weekend because it's my mum's 50th birthday and we're having a surprise party for her. I'll have to treat myself all weekend with a portable machine.

When I arrived at King's Cross, I realised there was industrial action on the tube and they were running every twenty minutes and were totally jam-packed. That is one thing I really don't miss about London. Give me Linthorpe Road in Middlesbrough any day.

SATURDAY 2 SEPTEMBER 1995

Strange feeling today because at 3pm I was having a pint with some friends and having a bet on the horses. Can't wait until next Saturday when we are playing again, I haven't won a bet all afternoon!

This mean and moody sho was taken by Bob Wilson's son Robert, for a book he did on goalkeepers. The front cover photo came from the same shoot at Ayresome Park. They are fantastic pictures, I was really impressed.

SUNDAY 3 SEPTEMBER 1995

Travelled back to Middlesbrough and met Terry McDermott, Kevin Keegan's assistant at Newcastle. We had a drink together and a good chat. He didn't comment too much on the foul on Jamie Pollock and the penalty claims, but he seems a very nice fellow.

MONDAY 4 SEPTEMBER 1995

I think it's going to be touch and go whether I'll be fit for Saturday. The groin is responding well to treatment but I think kicking is going to be a problem. I'll just have to keep my fingers crossed because I desperately want to play. Gary Walsh is pressing for a place and I don't want to give him a chance.

TUESDAY 5 SEPTEMBER 1995

Gordon McQueen, the reserve team boss, told us he's trying to give up smoking. He's managed four days but he can't sleep at night and has mood swings. After seeing big Gordon in a bad mood once, I think we had better try and slip him a few cigarettes! I wonder how long he can keep it up though he seems very serious about it. Nick Barmby has been selected for England tomorrow, let's hope he does really well.

WEDNESDAY 6 SEPTEMBER 1995

It now becomes apparent that I will be struggling for Saturday. The tear in my groin has repaired quite nicely but the problem is that I haven't trained for a week and, although it doesn't feel too bad, it's still not 100 per cent. If I were to play on Saturday, there would be no way I could train properly and I couldn't risk trying to kick a ball. If I went into the game, it would be with a doubt about my fitness. I could easily start the game and then, when kicking the first ball, rip by groin muscle again and be out for two to three months. At this stage I really don't think it is worth the risk, even though I don't want to miss any games. It's a very hard decision to make. I'll know more by Friday.

THURSDAY 7 SEPTEMBER 1995

Bob Ward has definitely ruled me out of Saturday's game at Bolton and also gave me little or no chance for Tuesday's game at home to Southampton. It's a big blow but not really a shock.

It gives Gary Walsh a chance to try and establish himself for at least two games. It will be interesting to see what happens when I'm fit again, hopefully for the game against Coventry.

SATURDAY 9 SEPTEMBER 1995

We drew 1-1 with Bolton today and really should have won the game. After a bad start when they scored after 23 minutes, we came more into the game and our second half performance was very good. We created some great chances, but didn't score until 20 minutes before the end. Craig Hignett scored the goal after good build up play by Nick Barmby.

I hope I'm not out of the team for too long because I didn't enjoy not being involved in the build up to the game, or after it, but I was glad I went and was with all the lads for the game.

Gary Walsh didn't have a great deal to do, but what he did do was OK.

SUNDAY 10 SEPTEMBER 1995

I was in for treatment again this morning and I was joined by Nigel Pearson who twisted his knee slightly yesterday. It's always a nightmare coming in on a Sunday and, to make things worse, I was totally p***ed off sitting in that medical room!

MONDAY 11 SEPTEMBER 1995

At last, for the first time, I could start doing some work today. Bob took me to Springs Health Club and worked me very hard on the step machines and different weight machines. I'm delighted because as well as getting some hard work under my belt, I had no reaction from my groin. Hopefully tomorrow, I can do some running and handling and get out of that treatment room for a couple of hours.

TUESDAY 12 SEPTEMBER 1995

Probably our most disappointing performance of the season so far - a 0-0 draw against Southampton. We never really looked like scoring. They probably had the best chances of the game with Gary Walsh making some good saves. He played well and that's going to make things hard for me. If he plays well and the team keeps getting results then it's going to be very difficult to win my place back. It's a nightmare not being involved. Another good crowd of 29,000 at the new stadium which is fantastic.

THURSDAY 14 SEPTEMBER 1995

Had a good session today with Mike Kelly and I was really pleased to get no reaction from my groin. My general fitness is still below par, but that won't take long to get back.

Bob still doesn't want me kicking any balls yet, and that means I probably won't be involved at the weekend. I'm disappointed but I know after training today I won't be match fit by then. I'm targeting next week to be totally fit and training properly.

After my experience of not being involved the last couple of games, it amazes me how people like Paul Wilkinson keep themselves going when they're not playing every week. It must be very depressing. I honestly think Wilko could still do a very good job for us, but I think the manager will always now overlook him. I hope he gets a good move soon because he deserves it.

FRIDAY 15 SEPTEMBER 1995

I definitely won't be involved this weekend and it now looks as though I will miss Wednesday's game for the simple reason that I haven't played for nearly 2½ weeks. I will now probably play in the reserve game at Hartlepool against Blackpool. Hopefully, if I come through that OK, I will be fit for selection the next Saturday against Manchester City. It will be interesting to see what the gaffer does.

Even though I've had only two days of proper training I felt pretty good today and know I'm only a few days' training from being fully fit.

Why is it whenever I don't play it's never windy? It's been amazingly still recently and I bet the next time I'm involved it will be blowing a gale!

SATURDAY 16 SEPTEMBER 1995

Another great result for us today - a 2-1 home win over Coventry - but it was a close thing. We actually came from behind in the second half with goals from Steve Vickers and Jan Fjortoft. We didn't start playing anywhere near as well as we can until after they scored. We are now ninth in the table.

I trained very hard this morning with Mike Kelly and the other reserve players. It went very well. My groin felt great and it's nice to be training properly again. It's a horrible feeling not being involved and watching the games on a Saturday. There's an empty feeling when the game finishes and you're not part of it, you even feel as if you don't deserve to have a beer in the players' lounge afterwards - though I normally do!

Who said Robbie Mustoe was a hard man? Sharing a joke for the cameras at a promotional event for Cellnet.

MONDAY 18 SEPTEMBER 1995

Another hard session under my belt today and at Springs in the afternoon. I'm feeling better all the time and it looks as though I will be playing in the reserve game on Thursday against Blackpool. If I come through that OK, I will be fit for selection at the weekend.

TUESDAY 19 SEPTEMBER 1995

I felt awful today - very heavy legged. I think I've probably overworked myself over the last few days, so I think I'll take it a bit easier for the next two days before the game on Thursday.

The team for tomorrow's cup game against Rotherham has two changes. Jaime Moreno replaces Craig Hignett and Phil Whelan comes in for Nigel Pearson, both of whom are being rested.

Watched the Celtic v Rangers match at Coxy's with him and Phil Whelan. We had a fiver each on the first goal scorer. Phil won (Ally McCoist). I think I'll give up betting - I can't remember the last time I won.

WEDNESDAY 20 SEPTEMBER 1995

We beat Rotherham 2-1 in the Coca-Cola Cup at the Riverside but it was a disappointing result. We should have won by more. It now makes our second leg away game a lot more difficult than it should have been. Robbie Mustoe scored the first goal after a great cross from Coxy. Jan Fjortoft scored the second after good work again from Nick Barmby.

Shock result of the night - Manchester United 0 York 3.

Had another bet on the game tonight - for the first goalscorer - but again no luck. After studying the form, my girlfriend Jo picked Robbie Mustoe to score first and us to win 3-1 at odds of 80-1. She only missed it by one goal. Perhaps I'll get her to pick my horses out in future and take her to Walthamstow dogs next time I go. "Go on the 2 dog".

THURSDAY 21 SEPTEMBER 1995

I played my first game back after injury tonight, a reserve game against Blackpool at Hartlepool. We won 3-0 but they caused us a few problems and worked very hard. It was good to be playing again and I had no reaction from my groin. Chris Freestone scored a hat-trick and has now scored nine goals already this season.

FRIDAY 22 SEPTEMBER 1995

Travelled with the squad to Manchester for our game against City tomorrow. I'm not sure whether I'll be on the bench or not. The Ryder Cup started today and after the first day we are 5-3 down.

SATURDAY 23 SEPTEMBER 1995

Another great result today - a 1-0 win. I must admit, City were absolutely awful but you still have to beat them and we did. Nick Barmby scored for us and had another good game. He's settled in very well. I think Manchester City will struggle to stay up this season. I saw Niall Quinn, an old team-mate at Arsenal, before the game and he said the atmosphere in their dressing room was terrible. We now move up to seventh in the league.

After the second day in the Ryder Cup we are trailing 9-7. Corey Pavin chipped in at the last to beat Faldo. It doesn't look too good for us. They have only got to get 14 points to retain the cup.

I never really played golf until I came to Middlesbrough. Coxy and a few of the other lads played and I got hooked. It's a great way of relaxing and getting away from the pressure. You're out on your own for three or four hours (or five the way I play).

When you play you can appreciate how good the pro's are. The Ryder Cup is like the World Cup for football and is a fabulous competition. It's great to watch. I just hope it doesn't turn out to be an easy win for the Americans.

SUNDAY 24 SEPTEMBER 1995

We won the Ryder Cup after winning 7½ of the 12 points. There were absolutely amazing scenes on the last hole when Philip Walton won the all important match. I watched it at Coxy's house and we were jumping around his living room like maniacs. I don't think anyone could have imagined the outcome of this yesterday. Even Seve Ballasteros was crying. Brilliant! It's going to be hard for any sporting event to top this in terms of excitement and drama this season.

MONDAY 25 SEPTEMBER 1995

I'm going to play in the reserve match at Grimsby tomorrow night and it will be good to get another game under my belt, but hopefully not too many reserve ones!

TUESDAY 26 SEPTEMBER 1995

We beat Grimsby 4-0 tonight and although it was a big winning margin, it was closer than it sounds. I was really pleased with the way I played and I think I'm now back to being 100 per cent fit again, although I still don't think I will be involved in the first team on Saturday.

A Miller's Tale

WEDNESDAY 27 SEPTEMBER 1995

Phil Whelan, Neil Cox and myself took advantage of our day off and went to Newcastle races. It was a good day out but, unfortunately, another lack of winners for all of us. Not content with that, we ended up at Cleveland Park to finish off our day with a bit of greyhound racing and we all fared better there.

THURSDAY 28 SEPTEMBER 1995

A lot of speculation in the papers again today that John Collins is coming to Middlesbrough. Some say he has already had talks with Bryan Robson but he has denied it. I think something will happen soon because Celtic have dropped him after he said he wanted to leave. £3 million will probably be enough. Let's hope he comes to us.

FRIDAY 29 SEPTEMBER 1995

I'm definitely not involved tomorrow so I'll train on my own with Mike Kelly in the morning. I'm a bit disappointed the gaffer didn't have a word with me about the situation. Maybe he'll say something tomorrow. I've just got to keep working hard and wait for my chance again. This is the first time I've really been left out since I joined the club and I can tell you it's not something I'm enjoying. It's the hardest thing I've had to contemplate in my career so far. Sometimes it's very hard not to get down and depressed, especially the longer it goes on. I hope we win tomorrow, I wouldn't want them to lose, even without me, but let's hope it's 5-4!

SATURDAY 30 SEPTEMBER 1995

Our great start continued today with another brilliant win, 2-0 over Blackburn, the reigning Premiership champions, although I must say they looked very tired after their European exploits in the week.

We are now only three points from the top of the table. It's an unbelievable start for us and everything at the club is buzzing. Nick Barmby scored the first with Craig Hignett getting the second and, although they both played very well, I thought Robbie Mustoe was magnificent. He's such an under-rated player.

Coxy and myself went to a new night-club in Stockton called Visage although, by the time we got there, it was more of a mirage! Enough said!

MONDAY 2 OCTOBER 1995

Trained at Ayresome Park today. All the squad was together preparing for the match against Rotherham tomorrow night. It's a tricky tie for us as they have scored an away goal, but, considering our defence is very tight at the moment, I think we'll go safely through.

The gaffer wasn't around today and nobody was willing to say where he was. Is John Collins finally coming?

TUESDAY 3 OCTOBER 1995

We beat Rotherham 1-0 with Steve Vickers scoring the important goal. It ended up as quite a comfortable win for us after they had a man sent off in the first half. Not a very inspiring game though.

The gaffer was again missing, so something very big is happening but it's still shrouded in some mystery.

The biggest mystery of the day, however, is how O. J. Simpson got a "not guilty" verdict at his murder trial. They're not even looking for any other suspects. Maybe that's where the gaffer is!

WEDNESDAY 4 OCTOBER 1995

I played in the reserves tonight and we beat Manchester City 1-0 to go top of the league. We played some great football.

There are some excellent players coming through and worth keeping your eye on - Mickey Barron, Wes Byrne, Craig Liddle, Philip Stamp, Keith O'Halloran, Chris Freestone. With the experience of Paul Wilkinson, John Hendrie and Clayton Blackmore alongside them, they are really beginning to shine.

FRIDAY 6 OCTOBER 1995

Trained this morning and it became apparent that Bryan Robson is in Brazil trying to sign Juninho for £4.75 million, but Arsenal are also said to be interested. What a signing he would be.

Played out on pitch today in the five-a-side and scored a hat-trick in two minutes. Maybe I'm in the wrong position! I actually started out playing as a right-winger when I was a kid and only went in goal because the keeper didn't turn up. I got man of the match and I've never looked back since.

Apparently Jim Platt when he was keeper at Boro, used to play up front for the reserves. He even got a hat-trick once! I should try that - it might be my best chance of getting back in!

SATURDAY 7 OCTOBER 1995

Had a good day out at York Races with Paul Wilkinson. Frankie Dettori had four winners and luckily we were on three of them.

Luckily enough, all the bar staff were from Middlesbrough so we were never waiting long for a drink. Got a tip for Wednesday at Haydock from an owner (Double Splendour) so watch this space!

SUNDAY 8 OCTOBER 1995

It was announced today that Juninho has signed for Boro for £4.75 million. It's absolutely amazing news and as big a shock for us players as it is for the fans - we didn't have a clue! Despite what people think, we don't get any inside information.

It's incredible to think we've spent over £10 million already this season, as well as having a new £16 million stadium. West Ham can't manage to scrape together £500,000. The stadium soon won't be big enough for the demand. It's very exciting times on Teesside. Long may it continue. It will be interesting to see how Juninho will cope with that biting North East wind in January! Juninho is a world class player and it just shows how ambitious this club is.

My girlfriend Jo had an audition for a job teaching aerobics at Springs this afternoon and was delighted when they offered her the job. I just hope she doesn't ask me to join in too many classes, I don't think I could keep up!

WEDNESDAY 11 OCTOBER 1995

Double Splendour won at 8-1 - what a tipster!

We played a friendly game against the local side, Billingham Town, tonight due to the fact that our youth team are using their facilities for their games. We all played half a game and I think we were pleased no-one picked up any injuries. England drew 0-0 with

Norway in what was a pretty poor game. Nick Barmby and Jan Fjortoft played against each other. Quite a few of the players and their wives or girlfriends went to the opening of another new club at the Tall Trees near Yarm. Besides waiting 20 minutes for a drink and losing half the people you came in with, it was very impressive.

THURSDAY 12 OCTOBER 1995

Had a day out at Redcar Races today along with Neil Cox, Phil Whelan and Paul Wilkinson. We all had a few winners and a good day. I spoke to Willie Ryan, the jockey (who's a big Arsenal fan), at the meeting and he had drink with us afterwards.

FRIDAY 13 OCTOBER 1995

All the lads are back today and it's good to have a full dressing room again. The gaffer pulled me over when I got in and said he wanted to see me after training.

As it happens I was running a bit late after training and, by the time I got round to seeing him, he had to go to a meeting. He said he will see me tomorrow at the hotel in Sheffield. The suspense is killing me.

In the afternoon I went to York with Jo to have a look around and do some shopping. I really like it there and I should imagine it's a lovely place to live.

Jamie Pollock damaged a rib in training today and could be doubtful for Sunday's game at Sheffield Wednesday.

SUNDAY 15 OCTOBER 1995

Our unbelievable start to the season continued and we climbed to fourth in the Premier League by beating Sheffield Wednesday 1-0 at Hillsborough. Quite remarkable. Craig Hignett scored his fourth goal of the season, from the penalty spot. Sheffield Wednesday are another team we have come up against who look completely out of sorts. We took advantage of this and for long periods had a lot of possession.

It's difficult for me to genuinely enjoy the after match celebrations. You're really happy for all your team mates and the club but it's so disappointing and frustrating not being involved in playing your part in the team's win. I feel as if I'm on a yo-yo at the moment. I try and keep myself bubbly and busy in the dressing room, but get quite low about the whole situation. The funny thing is I'm pleased the team are doing well but, because of this, it will probably mean I'm out of the team for longer. The manager said nothing to me again so I still don't know what's going on.

Jan Fjortoft came off injured and could be struggling for next Saturday. John Hendrie came on and did a very good job.

MONDAY 16 OCTOBER 1995

Juninho jetted into Teesside and the whole place has gone Samba mad. We'll meet him tomorrow at training. He looks tiny and reminds me of the jockey, Frankie Dettori.

TUESDAY 17 OCTOBER 1995

He does look like Frankie Dettori but I think Frankie might be slightly bigger than Juninho. He's the smallest footballer I've ever seen. In fact, he's the only player that the kit fits so he must be small. The

kit seems to get smaller every time it gets washed. For the bigger lads it's hopeless. In my first season the shorts were indecent sometimes!

I trained with the goalkeepers so didn't really watch him train but, according to the other lads, you could tell straight away that he's a quality player. Apparently his touch and vision were unbelievable in the five-a-side game. There are a few formalities to sort out before he can play but it shouldn't be too long.

The gaffer said nothing to me which was a bit disappointing but I'm sure he will. I suppose he's had a lot on his plate lately. I'm in the reserve game tomorrow night against Preston at Hartlepool and guess what? It's going to be windy again!

Frankie Dettori jets in! Only joking, Juninho flies in to set Teesside alight and send the fans into a Samba frenzy.

WEDNESDAY 18 OCTOBER 1995

We beat Preston 3-0. I haven't let a goal in yet in four reserve games - I hope that's not tempting fate. We had quite a young team out and they played very well with Chris Freestone getting another two goals.

THURSDAY 19 OCTOBER 1995

Visited Yarm Fair in the evening and had my palm read by Gypsy Rose Lee in her caravan. She said I was going to lose weight but not through an illness. That's the best bit of news I've had for a long time, although I hope it's got nothing to do with a certain grey-haired goalkeeping coach!

FRIDAY 20 OCTOBER 1995

It looks as though Jan will be fit for Saturday so we will probably be unchanged. Phil Whelan came into training with a big black donkey jacket on and instantly had the Mickey taken out of him. He laughed it off but what he didn't know was that someone had put a big sticker on the back with Middlesbrough Borough Council on it. He left without realising and was probably walking around Middlesbrough all afternoon with it plastered on his back. It couldn't happen to a nicer fellow.

Ben Roberts has gone on loan to Hartlepool for a month. It's a good move for him, not only because it's first team football, but it's still local. I think he will do very well. I rang him this evening to wish him all the best and he seemed fairly confident.

SATURDAY 21 OCTOBER 1995

The gaffer had a word with me before today's game with QPR. He talked about my situation and said just to keep training hard and wait for my chance again. He said I had been very unlucky getting injured after starting the season well.

I'm glad he's finally said something to me, it shows he appreciates that I am still part of the team. I was starting to feel forgotten and you wonder whether you're ever going to get another chance. It's easy to let things get on top of you and doubts start filling your mind. I feel a bit more reassured.

The team is playing well and Walshy is doing a good job so, realistically, there is no way I can get into the team right now. There's no reason for the gaffer to change things. It's frustrating but I've just got to bide my time.

We got another good win today - 1-0 against QPR - Europe here we come! It wasn't the best of games. Craig Hignett scored again from the penalty spot but I couldn't understand why, when we were awarded another penalty, Jan took it instead of Higgy and consequently missed. I don't think the manager was best pleased.

SUNDAY 22 OCTOBER 1995

I came second in the golf today which is a lot better than the last time I played, trailing in last.

Neil Cox won £2,500 on an £8 horse bet on Saturday. Normally we go halves each on any betting so I rang him and said I'd give him my £4 tomorrow morning. I somehow doubt whether he'll hand over £1,250 to me though. You know who your friends are when money's involved!

MONDAY 23 OCTOBER 1995

I heard today from John Bundy, a good friend of mine who I used to regularly drink with in London. He told me his daughter, Hannah, had died this afternoon from cancer. She was only 19.

I got to know the family well when I was in London. John had three daughters and even then Hannah was suffering from cancer. She got the all-clear and everything seemed alright. Then it came back. She battled against it but eventually she lost the fight. She was such a gentle, lovely person.

It really puts life in perspective. I'm worried about not playing and so on and then something like this happens. My problems are nothing compared to what Hannah went through and what has happened to John's family. I'm incredibly lucky to be doing what I am and just to be healthy. It really makes you realise that we should all stop moaning about things and get on and enjoy life. It's not a dress rehearsal.

I feel very sorry for John, Caroline and their family and hope they can be strong together and come through this as best they can. God bless, Hannah.

WEDNESDAY 24 OCTOBER 1995

Flew down to London this morning and checked into the Seldon Park Hotel. When we got there, we found out there were only seven rooms available. That meant the ones who weren't involved - myself, Clayton Blackmore and Jaime Moreno - had to sit all afternoon in the same room we had lunch in. I couldn't believe it. Luckily enough, we had a Mega Drive with us and we played the PGA golf game all afternoon. By the time 6pm came I'd been playing that long I reckon I could have got into the Ryder Cup team.

In the game against Palace, we fell behind twice early in the match but came back to draw 2-2 and force a replay. We must play better back at the Riverside. Craig Hignett scored again as well as Nicky Barmby. We travelled back to Manchester in the evening by coach and I didn't get to sleep until 3.30am. I feel absolutely knackered!

THURSDAY 25 OCTOBER 1995

I didn't get up until 1pm today and that was only because we had to go down for lunch where I had steak, chips and onion rings. It wasn't exactly good preparation for tonight's reserve game at Rotherham.

We set off in two cars to Rotherham. Myself, the gaffer, Clayton, Jaime and Craig Liddle were all involved. We drew 1-1 but all the lads who travelled looked shattered, myself included. I couldn't wait to get back to Manchester and get to bed. I wish I hadn't had those onion rings - they kept repeating on me during the second half.

FRIDAY 26 OCTOBER 1995

Trained at the hotel for tomorrow's match at Manchester United. Played the golf game again in the evening. I beat Coxy, Jaime and Clayton and won "$60,000". Not bad for a night's work.

SATURDAY 27 OCTOBER 1995

Old Trafford is never an easy place to get a result so, when Roy Keane was sent off after 20 minutes, I felt we missed a good opportunity to get something from the match. They scored towards the end of each half with old boy Gary Pallister getting the first goal. We should have had a penalty in the second half but lost 2-0.

MONDAY 30 OCTOBER 1995

Juninho trained with us again today - he still hasn't grown any bigger. The club are hoping that they receive all his papers by the weekend so he can play against Leeds. All the players are going out for a drink tomorrow after training to celebrate the birth of Jaime's baby boy and they're going to take Juninho with them. I can't go because I'm going to Hannah's funeral on Wednesday but, knowing them, Juninho will only be worth £50,000 by Wednesday morning - if he's lucky!

TUESDAY 31 OCTOBER 1995

Trained this morning at Ayresome Park, then it was straight to Darlington to catch the train to London. I'd forgotten about traffic jams but was soon reminded when I was stuck in a taxi in the rush hour in Walthamstow. That's one thing I definitely don't miss. It was good to see my family again and I had a drink with John Bundy. It's Hannah's funeral tomorrow and it's a terrible time for him.

WEDNESDAY 1 NOVEMBER 1995

A very emotional day today at the funeral service. You find out who your real friends are at times like this. I was just glad to have been able to go. At least now Hannah is no longer suffering from her illness.

Got the train back to Darlington in the evening.

THURSDAY 2 NOVEMBER 1995

Phil Whelan today had a face like a balloon. It was the funniest thing I'd seen for ages. When he walked into the treatment room everybody was in stitches laughing. He looked like the Elephant Man. Maybe that's a bit harsh on John Merrick!

I managed to borrow a camera from Lynne, the kit lady, and took a picture when he wasn't looking. He wasn't happy.

We found out tonight that Phil has broken his jaw. I can't believe it. He'll obviously miss Saturday's game, as will Coxy and Derek Whyte, so it's going to cause the gaffer a headache over team selection. Maybe Craig Liddle will play.

Juninho received his clearance to play and the gaffer says he will definitely play on Saturday. The way things are going he could play at the back!

FRIDAY 3 NOVEMBER 1995

I didn't train today because I've got a slight calf strain and thought it was better to rest and train tomorrow with Mike Kelly.

Craig Liddle is going to make his league debut tomorrow, replacing Neil Cox at right back. We are also playing a flat back four for the first time this season because of all the injuries.

SATURDAY 4 NOVEMBER 1995

We got a 1-1 draw with Leeds - overall, not a bad result. We played well in the first half, but they had the better second half. Juninho had a very good debut and set up our goal, scored by Jan Fjortoft, who also looked sharp. I was impressed with how Juninho reacted when he was clattered a couple of times - he just got straight back up and carried on. Although he did get himself booked - naughty boy!

SUNDAY 5 NOVEMBER 1995

Coxy, myself and our girlfriends had our own fireworks display in the gardens where we live. Coxy was very quick away from the fireworks after lighting them. I thought he was injured!

MONDAY 6 NOVEMBER 1995

The gaffer pulled me out of tonight's reserve game at Leicester because Gary Walsh was sick during training. I think he'll be OK but you never know, this could be my chance. Nick Barmby is also doubtful after hurting his Achilles. At this rate, I'll be playing up front before I get a chance in goal. There are now 11 first team players injured so it's going to be a testing time for us. I think the gaffer may have to play on Wednesday against Palace.

John Pickering asked me today how I was and I said OK. He said he was pleased that I wasn't moping around and had managed to remain in fairly high spirits when around the club, even though I was still not playing. I just said: "It's a long season and we all play our part and we're in this together". I appreciated him asking me and he did seem genuinely interested.

TUESDAY 7 NOVEMBER 1995

More frustration for me today as I had to drop out of training after aggravating a calf problem I've had for a few days. I've gone from being in the frame for a recall to being back on the treatment table. When's it all going to end? I'm having a really hard time trying to remain patient.

A Miller's Tale

WEDNESDAY 8 NOVEMBER 1995

We beat Palace 2-0 - a great result considering the amount of injuries we've had. Craig Hignett and Jan Fjortoft scored the goals, although Higgy picked up a foot injury. We dominated most of the game, apart from a spell near half time when Gary Walsh had to make a couple of very good saves.

It's difficult because you want the team to win first and foremost but you know the only way you are going to get a chance is if a goal goes in or people make mistakes. I will always acknowledge a good save but it's a Catch 22. I tell Gary "Well done", and I mean it, but deep down every time he makes a good save I'm thinking "Oh, S**t".

Looking particularly sprightly for this training session. I was obviously a bit under the weather - or was it just a hard night out the evening before?

Three good friends of mine came up from London for the game and we had a good night out afterwards. It must have been good because Chas 'n' Dave ended up on the CD player in the restaurant. That's when I realised it was time to go home.

THURSDAY 9 NOVEMBER 1995

I'm pleased my old friend Alan Smith got a crowd of 17,000 for his benefit game at Arsenal. He deserves it. Meanwhile, I was on the treatment table with this calf injury.

FRIDAY 10 NOVEMBER 1995

We had a roll call at training this morning to see who is available and fit to play against Sampdoria tomorrow in the game to officially open the new stadium. Juninho will definitely play and was in training today. I won't be fit enough to take part which is unfortunate. I think we could have done without this game because of the injuries we've got and also the replay last Wednesday, but hopefully it'll be a great occasion.

SATURDAY 11 NOVEMBER 1995

It always seems that the atmosphere at the club is a bit subdued when the lads are away on international duty. But it is a measure of how far the club has come that so many players are now being selected for their countries.

I'm sure as the season continues there will be many more. Eire have called up Chris Morris to face Portugal next week. Great news for him.

SUNDAY 12 NOVEMBER 1995

A crowd of 10,000 turned up to see the 0-0 draw with Sampdoria. It was a bit of a disappointing turnout and I think the club should have given some tickets cheaply to local schools or something. It would have meant there was a larger crowd. And, more importantly, a lot of kids who don't get the chance to see games normally would be able to see the new stadium and players such as Juninho. A chance missed, I feel. Juninho looked very sharp and created a chance for the gaffer which he duly fluffed. Went out in the evening with Neil Cox, Gordon McQueen and our girlfriends/wives.

A Miller's Tale

MONDAY 13 NOVEMBER 1995

Phil Whelan came in today for the first time since his jaw had been wired up. He has lost 11lb in weight already and you can tell as well. God knows what he'll lose after another four weeks with it on.

TUESDAY 14 NOVEMBER 1995

Trained for the first time this morning and did a relatively gentle session with Ben Roberts. Everything went OK until virtually the last couple of balls when I felt a pain in my calf again. I couldn't believe it. After walking it off, it felt a bit better so I decided not to say anything to Bob Ward. I just got a massage on it and I hope it will settle down for tomorrow's training. I don't know if I'm doing the right thing, but I'm fed up being injured and sometimes you have to get on with it. Time will tell, especially when Mike Kelly comes back from the England squad (he's goalkeeping coach for the national squad) on Thursday and we start training very hard again.

WEDNESDAY 15 NOVEMBER 1995

Got through training OK today. We did some shooting with John Pickering while most of the first team lads were off.

THURSDAY 16 NOVEMBER 1995

Jan's place in the dressing room at Ayresome took a hammering from Nigel Pearson's marker pen after Norway failed to qualify for the European Championships. Unfortunately, he's not in until tomorrow. The lads even made up a dummy and hung it from the ceiling by his place. I'm not sure how he will take it.

Because we're not playing at Ayresome anymore, and it's going to be knocked down, Nigel has been doing caricatures and pictures whenever anything happens. It's always a good laugh to see what he's put up but I wonder what people think when they come into the dressing room.

FRIDAY 17 NOVEMBER 1995

Woke up this morning to a blanket of snow on the ground. It was absolutely freezing. The weather has definitely turned. Juninho came into the dressing room looking like an Eskimo, he had that many clothes on. Jan took Nigel's joke very well, but then again I don't think he had much choice.

SATURDAY 18 NOVEMBER 1995

We managed a 0-0 draw at Wimbledon but it was a game we had a good chance of winning. I don't think Wimbledon are the team they once were. There were no really great chances at either end - it wasn't exactly a classic. A couple of years ago a point at Wimbledon would have been a good result, but today we were disappointed not to come away with all three.

Juninho played well in parts but probably had his quietest game so far for us. The gaffer didn't play, instead Phil Stamp and Craig Liddle played in midfield and Coxy returned at right back. Stampy played particularly well. We had flown down to London so we were back on Teesside by 8pm.

Went out with Coxy in the evening. We always get people coming up to us and mostly they just want to talk about football. When things aren't going right, especially if they've had a few drinks, then they can say a few things but you have to put up with it. It's nice to be recognised, I take it as a compliment.

MONDAY 20 NOVEMBER 1995

Trained today with Mike Kelly again and I felt quite good. The calf injury held up and hopefully I've seen the last of it.

I weighed myself today and I've lost 4lb in two weeks which I'm really pleased about. It's in my best interests to keep as fit as I can. I'm going to train tomorrow morning as I've been told I'm not on the bench for the game against Spurs. It's funny because when I was at Arsenal I got the hump always being on the bench. Now, after being involved in the first team for so long and having been out for a while, it was nice on Saturday just to be involved again, even if it was just on the bench. I think I prefer that to sitting in the stand but, at the end of the day, I'm desperate to be playing again, otherwise I just feel like part of the fixtures and fittings. I can't understand how certain players are happy just to be a squad player and play every now and then.

I hope we beat Spurs tomorrow. Even though I'm no longer at Arsenal, it's still nice to beat the old enemy, the same as Newcastle and Sunderland now.

TUESDAY 21 NOVEMBER 1995

We lost 1-0 to Spurs. It was a really disappointing result for us and the performance was probably our worst at home so far. We never really looked like scoring in what was quite a poor game. Before they scored we had about 10 to 15 minutes of good possession and pressure but, unfortunately, we didn't take advantage of it. We fell to the old sucker punch and were caught on the break. Armstrong scored the goal though everybody, bar the linesman, thought it was offside. Chris Morris was booked which means he's suspended now. Neil Cox also picked up another booking that leaves him and Nigel Pearson one booking away from suspension. We're running out of defenders so perhaps Gordon McQueen will have to dust down his boots!

Jamie Pollock also picked up a nasty injury, a badly gashed head. He had about 12 stitches and he'll be struggling for Saturday.

WEDNESDAY 22 NOVEMBER 1995

I played for the reserves against Barnsley and we got another very good result for Gordon, winning 4-1. It means we are still top of the league. We could have had seven or eight really and we were unfortunate to concede a goal, our first at home. It was my first game for a while and I was fairly pleased, even though I didn't have loads to do. The lads played very well and John Hendrie, Alan Moore and Jaime Moreno came through the game OK.

THURSDAY 23 NOVEMBER 1995

A fairly quiet day today except for Chubby Brown popping into the dressing room after training - never a quiet event that.

There was a Miss Great Britain event being held at the stadium tonight and we were asked this morning if one of us could judge the competition. There weren't many takers as I think it would have gone down like a lead balloon with the wives and girlfriends! Maybe Chubby would have done it.

SATURDAY 25 NOVEMBER 1995

Middlesbrough 2 Liverpool 1 - a cracker of a game and a very important result for us. Neil Cox scored his first goal of the season after just two minutes and in the process won me £170. I had a tenner on him to score the first goal. We played really well in the first half, especially the front three who linked up brilliantly. Jamie Pollock also had a great game but I thought Craig Liddle was magnificent in defence and was my man of the match. Neil Ruddock equalised before Nick Barmby scored a great goal to put us back in front.

I was doing the commentary for Century Radio and there was an incident when Gary Walsh handled the ball outside the area. As soon as it happened I thought this is it, this is my chance to get back in. I didn't say much on the radio but I thought he was definitely going to be sent off. I didn't want him to be sent off but when the ref produced a yellow card it was still a body blow. It would have resulted in a three match ban for Gary if it was red. How's my luck?

MONDAY 27 NOVEMBER 1995

Trained at Ayresome Park today and, afterwards the gaffer said I could go to the Middlesbrough Supporters South gathering in London after the game at QPR on Saturday. The club will put myself and Coxy up in a hotel overnight and the gaffer said I could have Monday off. You can't turn that down, can you? I also got a tax rebate this morning so it had been a very enjoyable day until I played golf in the afternoon with Phil Whelan, Ben Roberts and Jaime Moreno. Phil and myself lost on the last hole when Phil missed a 6ft putt. Had to keep an eye on Jaime, he kept having a problem keeping a count of how many shots he'd had. It must be something to do with the exchange rate with Bolivia.

TUESDAY 28 NOVEMBER 1995

Found out today that Tony Donnelley, the old kit man at Arsenal, has died of cancer. He was obviously a lot older than Hannah, my friend's daughter who died earlier this month, but it is still a shock.

I always remember when I was an apprentice at Arsenal and I had to sweep and mop the hallways. Tony made me come in on a Sunday. I came in all the way on the tube but as soon as I got there he would say: "You can go home now, at least you got up early".

But the longer you were there, the more you got to respect him and he used to really look after you. He was brilliant at the job. The funny thing was that he never knew anyone by name; it was always by numbers. Even if it was Ian Wright or Tony Adams it was always "Oi you, number 13".

I spent a lot of time with Tony in my last three years at the club and we used to go to Walthamstow dogs together. It was always a good night out. From being really angry with him for making me come in on Sundays when I first started, we eventually became good friends. I'm glad I got a chance to see him again not long ago. He wasn't looking too well, in fact I almost walked past him, but it was good to see him.

I'm devastated because I can't go to the funeral tomorrow as we have a Coca-Cola Cup game at home to Birmingham. I'll be thinking of him though. "Go on the two dog". God bless, Tony.

WEDNESDAY 29 NOVEMBER 1995

A very frustrating game for us tonight. Birmingham put a lot of bodies behind the ball, especially in the second half, and it was hard to break them down. To be fair to them, they did it well. Juninho was great on the night and was unlucky not to score when he hit the bar with a magnificent free kick. In fairness, Gary Walsh had to make some very good saves at times to keep it at 0-0.

It all adds up to a very tricky replay at St Andrew's, but we have the advantage because they didn't score an away goal. I was on the bench tonight and it was much better than sitting in the stands, though I couldn't help thinking about Tony's funeral today. My thoughts were definitely with him.

Had a drink in Yarm 85, a wine bar in Yarm, and had a chat with Malcolm Allison whose former clubs include Middlesbrough. When I told my Dad, he was thrilled because Big Mal was his idol when I was a lad.

THURSDAY 30 NOVEMBER 1995

Had a practice game today and it brought home to me just how many players are in the same boat as me - Curtis Fleming, John Hendrie, Clayton Blackmore, Paul Wilkinson, Jaime Moreno and Phil Whelan. Except for Phil, all the rest were in last year's team. It just shows that you can not afford to be out of the team for any reasons because it's hard getting back in. Trust me, I know.

FRIDAY 1 DECEMBER 1995

We had a meeting this morning and the gaffer drummed it into us that we must not sit back on our good start. He said we've got to keep working hard and not get sloppy. It's too easy to relax and undo the good work we've done so far. If we keep going like this, who knows what we can achieve. I felt very low in training today, not that anybody would have known. I don't really know why it was, because I was alright when I started. Sometimes the reality of not playing and missing out on all the big games just hits me. I feel I'm wasting precious time and just wonder to myself how much longer I can keep myself mentally right about the situation. I know I must be patient and be ready physically and mentally when I get my chance, but will I get another one?

SATURDAY 2 DECEMBER 1995

We drew 1-1 with QPR at Loftus Road - a good result for us, a bad one for them. Jan Fjortoft was left out and Jaime Moreno took his place. I'm not quite sure if he was dropped or rested but surely you don't rest players at this time of the season. They missed a penalty early in the game and so did we but, luckily enough, Chris Morris scored the rebound. Our defence put in another great display and Gary Walsh had to make a couple of important saves.

Neil Cox, Curtis Fleming, Derek Whyte and myself went to the Middlesbrough Supporters South do in the evening and had a good night. Went out in London afterwards.

Mixing with the stars at the Middlesbrough Supporters South do in London. Dervla Kirwan from the TV show, Goodnight Sweetheart, whose boyfriend is a Boro supporter, is pictured with me, Coxy and Derek. Not sure where Coxy's hand is though.

A Miller's Tale

MONDAY 4 DECEMBER 1995

Took Coxy for 'Pie & Mash' in London today which he didn't mind too much. I told him you put loads of vinegar on it but he wouldn't have it. He finished it all but drew the line when I mentioned jellied eels!

TUESDAY 5 DECEMBER 1995

Trained at Tollesby Road in Middlesbrough today instead of Ayresome Park and it was a bog. You couldn't stand up. I think when we leave Ayresome we will struggle to get any quality training there. We like to try and play on the floor a lot, so will it affect our performances?

Playing in the reserves tomorrow night at Blackpool and it's bloody freezing.

WEDNESDAY 6 DECEMBER 1995

Derek Whyte and Curtis Fleming played their long awaited comeback matches in tonight's reserve team game and both came through it OK. Derek might have to play left back on Saturday as Chris Morris is suspended. I'm sure Derek feels he could have done with another game.

We won 4-2 and it was a positive performance but the only down side was that Higgy got booked. He's now suspended for the games against Birmingham and West Ham.

I was pleased with my performance. I must keep my attitude right because it's too easy to get p***ed off and not bother when you're in the reserves for a long spell.

We did well to make it home as the A66 was nearly blocked with snow on the way back. We contemplated pulling into the nearest pub for the night but we just managed to get through. Gordon McQueen was devastated!

THURSDAY 7 DECEMBER 1995

I decided not to train today and instead went to Springs for a light work out and swim. I know Mike Kelly will be fuming. He feels you should always train on a Thursday but I felt very tired this morning after last night's game and the travelling. I know I'll be training hard tomorrow and almost certainly on Saturday. They keep telling us that rest is part of training - unless you're a goalkeeper, I suppose.

FRIDAY 8 DECEMBER 1995

Surprise, surprise! Mike came in growling and in a mood and called me "part-time". Sometimes I think it gets personal as far as I am concerned because he's been my coach before, when I was at Lilleshall at the age of 14, and he makes an example of me. I train very hard and I know my attitude is good, even now when I'm out of the side. I never take liberties and feel I don't deserve his criticism.

After training I asked him whether or not he would be in tomorrow so I could train. He replied: "It's up to you, you're the one who picks and chooses when you want to train". I couldn't believe it. I told him to shove it and that I would train on my own at Springs.

Just before I left, I saw the manager and he told me I wasn't on the bench tomorrow. He caught me at a bad time and I vented my anger at Mike to him. I told him in no uncertain terms that I wouldn't be training with Mike tomorrow and the reasons why. I'm not sure it was the right thing to do but it just happened. I just let all of my frustrations out.

The gaffer told me again that I must be fit and ready for when I get my chance. He told me that Mike was only doing it because he felt he needed to push me.

He also said that I must play well in reserve games because "you never know who's watching!" I couldn't believe it. It was the first time that leaving Middlesbrough had ever entered my mind. It was like a big door slamming in my face - the realisation that it may at some stage come to that.

I really hope not because I'm desperate to stay here and get back in the team. I love it here. I've won promotion and I like the players and the people. It really upset me to think I might have to move on to get regular football or for whatever reason.

Football is a precarious business, one minute everything can be fine and the next you can be on your way or on the injury list, but it still came as a bit of a shock to think that I might be leaving.

SATURDAY 9 DECEMBER 1995

I spoke to the gaffer first thing today and said I wanted to take back what I had said about Mike. I thought about it long and hard last night and felt maybe I was wrong. I told him it was a heat of the moment thing. He said he was pleased I saw him and said he would prefer I had some sort of reaction because it showed I cared about the situation.

I trained with Mike this morning and I'm glad I did. His training is brilliant and I know he's keeping on at me for a reason. I know he has my best interests at heart even if it's hard to appreciate some times.

A game of two halves against Manchester City today. They started very well and deserved their lead. We came back well and it was important for us to get a goal back before half time, courtesy of

Nick Barmby. In the second half we were in a different class. Nick scored a second and Phil Stamp scored a great goal. But the goal of the day was Juninho's, simply because it was his first for the club. Stampy made the goal with a great shot and, for me, he was man of the match. Saying that, Gary Walsh had to make at least a couple of excellent saves. We're now fourth in the League. It's really incredible.

Uwe Fuchs met us in the evening after playing for Millwall against Sunderland. Unfortunately, they lost 6-0.

SUNDAY 10 DECEMBER 1995

Player's Christmas day out. We met at the Black Bull in Yarm then went on to the George and Dragon where we had a good laugh and sing-song. We eventually ended up at The Dickens pub in Middlesbrough. It was a great day out. It was just a shame we had to have it on Sunday rather than in the week because of the Birmingham replay.

TUESDAY 12 DECEMBER 1995

Frank Sinatra's 80th birthday today. Happy birthday Francis Albert!

I grew up with Frank Sinatra - my Dad loved him and I've got signed pictures - so this was a special day for me. Whenever we have a karaoke, the Sinatra songs always come out when it's my turn. If I didn't have a karaoke machine I'd be rubbish. Other than that, of course, I'm brilliant!

Coxy and myself attended a book signing session at W. H. Smiths, then did some Christmas shopping.

The fantastic scenes after the Luton game - the last at Ayresome Park at the end of the 1994-95 season. The victory made promotion all but certain and it was an incredible atmosphere. Derek Whyte has his player of the year award and Steve Vickers and I joined in the celebrations.

Training at Ayresome Park. Juninho and Kav look on as we try a flat back four system. The defence was looking particularly wooden on that day!

Out on the pitch for the five-a-side and showing the outfield lads up (or not, as the case may be). All goalkeepers are frustrated centre-forwards and I'm caught on camera showing off my lack of silky skills with Coxy and Steve Vickers.

Norway are out of Euro 96 and this is our sympathetic way of cheering Jan Fjortoft up! Nigel Pearson and John Hendrie show off our mock hanging and the box at John's feet has a compassionate message for Jan - "Jan, please stand on this then we'll kick it away!"

John Hendrie always wears the worst gear and he turned up with this dodgy "Big Mal" coat one day for training. It has to be the worst jacket I've ever seen.

Viv Anderson and the drag artist 'Crystal Starr' perform their double act during the Tenerife trip. I think he/she definitely liked him.

... and the lads watch on. Judging by this picture, Viv's efforts were clearly much appreciated by Neil Cox.

MILLER TIM

Main Pic: Another one that got away.
Or was it a fantastic finger-tip save?

Top right: One of the pitfalls of playing
football - training on Christmas Day. It was
a really happy picture, little were we to
know that we were about to lose 4-0 on
Boxing Day and go on a horrendous run of
eight successive league defeats.

Bottom right: John Hendrie set up his
Santa's Grotto for Christmas Day. He even
found a little boy to sit on his knee!

Jaime, Curtie, Kav and Coxy catch some sun during the Tenerife trip. Jaime looks more used to than Kav. This was the day after John Hendrie's infamous eyebrow shaving incident.

Here's me trying to motivate the troops with a few smoke signals.

Juninho, Jaime Moreno and I waving goodbye to Ayresome Park. The last day we spent at the old place before the bulldozers moved in and a fond farewell to a ground with some good memories.

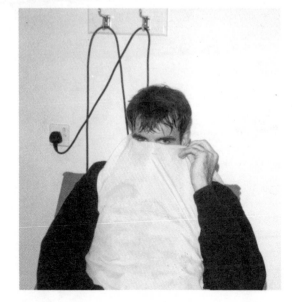

Phil Whelan tries to disguise his face after breaking his jaw.

The evening after the Manchester United game and the end of the season. My family - my dad John, my brother Gary and mother Val - came up to celebrate my dad's 60th birthday.

Looking forward to the new season with the First Division championship trophy. A great achievement for us and a proud moment for me. Shame about the haircut though!

WEDNESDAY 13 DECEMBER 1995

Played for the reserves tonight against Grimsby - we won 2-1. I was disappointed with my performance although the conditions were awful. We're now about six points clear with a game in hand.

THURSDAY 14 DECEMBER 1995

Trained in the morning, then me and Coxy visited a school this afternoon. The reaction we get is always amazing, the kids have gone Boro mad, we're like heroes. You can't see this sort of thing as a chore because you have to put it back in. When you see the expressions on the kids' faces and realise how much it means to them, it's really worthwhile.

It's nice to give the kids goals and someone to look up to. If it makes them want to go and do it then it has had a positive effect. When I was a kid, my heroes were Pat Jennings and Peter Shilton. I'll never forget when I was a schoolboy and I saw Peter Shilton playing, it really inspired me.

Jamie looks as if he's struggling for Saturday with a sore knee. There's also bad news for Robbie Mustoe - he has had an exploratory knee operation. He can't seem to shake off the injury. I know he's not happy with it.

FRIDAY 15 DECEMBER 1995

We travelled to Blackburn this afternoon. Jamie is definitely not playing. The good news is that Curtis Fleming is back in the squad and will probably play at left back. Craig Liddle will move into midfield.

Nigel Pearson and myself had a nightmare trying to get to sleep tonight. We were above the disco at the hotel. We might as well have been down there. I'm sure every time we complained they turned the music up.

SATURDAY 16 DECEMBER 1995

Blackburn beat us 1-0 and it was another game where we could have got something. We never got going in the first half and went behind to a brilliant Alan Shearer goal just before half-time. We played a lot better in the second half but never really looked like scoring. Derek Whyte was sent off in the last minute and will now miss the Forest game. Graeme le Saux broke his ankle in a dreadful accident whilst challenging Juninho. Juninho came into the game more as it went on and showed some neat touches second half. Our defence was again outstanding. We also had great support from our travelling fans who were there in their thousands.

MONDAY 18 DECEMBER 1995

After training today, all the apprentices had to do their Christmas show to earn the Christmas money they get for doing the boots all year. It's an MFC tradition and if they didn't sing, they didn't get any money. They ranged from excellent - The Proclaimers - to rank - Boyzone. The Boyzone impersonators consequently had to strip and run around the Ayresome Park pitch absolutely starkers. Very amusing! Juninho seemed to enjoy it, but I don't think he could quite believe what was going on. It's obviously not something that happens over in Brazil!

I had to pull out of the reserve game tonight. I really felt rough. I didn't feel too good in training this morning but I thought I would be OK. When I arrived at Hartlepool, I knew I was struggling. I saw

Gordon, explained the situation, and luckily enough Danny, the apprentice goalkeeper, was there, so I lent him my gloves, boots and shin-pads and then went straight home. I don't think he could believe it. I hope he does OK. Mind you, if he has a blinder, it will be another team I won't be able to get into. The gaffer was down for a rare appearance as well to keep him on his toes just in case he's needed over the busy Christmas period.

TUESDAY 19 DECEMBER 1995

Still felt a bit groggy today and I was sent home when I turned up for training. All the other lads travelled to Birmingham. I'm hoping to make the journey early tomorrow morning after having another day in bed.

WEDNESDAY 20 DECEMBER 1995

Birmingham 2 Boro 0. A nightmare result for us. We let in two bad goals early in the game and it was always going to be a struggle to reverse the score. It wasn't through want of trying, but we don't look like scoring bundles of goals at the moment. If you look back, we've won most of our games when we've kept a clean sheet. We don't let many goals in, but on the other hand we don't score many either. Norwich won their game and we would have played them in the quarter-finals. We would have fancied our chances to progress into the semi-final but it wasn't to be.

We didn't get back to Middlesbrough until 1.30 am. It always seems to take longer when you lose.

THURSDAY 21 DECEMBER 1995

Had a swim and a massage at Springs today and the mood is a bit sombre in the camp after last night's result. We've just got to get on with it and turn it around with a good performance and result against West Ham on Saturday.

Went shopping in York this afternoon. It's a great place, but all the little streets look the same. I kept coming back to the same shop every time - unless there are 15 French Connections in York!

FRIDAY 22 DECEMBER 1995.

John Hendrie walked into training with an old 70's style, sheepskin jacket (Malcolm Allison type thing). He wears the worst gear I've ever seen. I had to take a picture just to prove it to people. He takes the stick well though.

It poured down during training today and the pitch was waterlogged. This is after being frozen solid the day before. I bet Juninho has never seen so many climate changes in one week. He seems to be coping OK though.

SATURDAY 23 DECEMBER 1995

Juninho was in a different class today and ran the show from midfield as we beat West Ham 4-2. He set up goals for Jan Fjortoft and Neil Cox. Chris Morris scored a great header from an excellent ball in from Coxy and John Hendrie scored his first goal of the season late on, which was good to see. It was another good performance and their two goals were only consolation efforts really. Coxy picked up a late booking which means he will miss the cup game against Notts County and the Arsenal match at home.

We had our club Christmas party tonight and it went well. I was sat on the last table by the exit, and I think that was only because of a late cancellation. When you're out, you're out!

Gordon McQueen told me a great story about when he went out with the coaching staff yesterday. His wife dropped him off in Yarm in the afternoon. She was driving her new BMW for the first time. When she returned to pick him and John Pickering up late in the evening, Gordon was saying how nice the new car was, how much room there was and how quiet the engine was, only for his wife to turn round and say: "You stupid idiot, this is your car"! Must have been a good afternoon.

SUNDAY 24 DECEMBER 1996

No training today and a fairly quiet day all round. Had a couple of drinks with Neil Cox and his girlfriend in the evening. That's the only thing about being a footballer. It's great for the majority of the time except Christmas because of so many games and training in between. You very rarely go out at Christmas until it's actually over. Still, I wouldn't change a thing.

MONDAY 25 DECEMBER 1996

Christmas Day and we trained at 10.30am at Ayresome Park. The pitch was frozen after a heavy frost overnight so we were restricted to some gentle running. Most of the players were delighted we trained this morning because originally we were going to train at 6.00pm and then travel to a Liverpool hotel for tomorrow's game at Everton. Now we're flying in the morning so we could spend Christmas day with our families.

TUESDAY 26 DECEMBER 1995

Our worst result and performance of the season - we lost 4-0 to Everton. We just seemed all over the place today and, to make matters worse, we lost Derek Whyte and Chris Morris through injury and Jamie Pollock was booked and is now suspended.

It was a bad day all round. When our plane was just about to land, we were told we had to circle the airport so they could de-ice the runway. Then, on the way to the game, the coach managed to hit a stationary car when it skidded on black ice. To make matters worse, on arriving at Goodison, our kit hadn't turned up and didn't arrive until 2.15pm

John Hendrie gets into the festive spirit for Christmas Day training. He obviously put on a bit of weight with too much Christmas cheer - or was it just a cushion up his jumper?

THURSDAY 28 DECEMBER 1995

We had to train at Redcar beach today and it was freezing. It must be cold up here because even the beach is under snow. It was -15°C last night and I don't think it was much warmer at Redcar today. The other lads trained in the (warm) gym at Ayresome Park. The game at Forest on Saturday will definitely be on as they have installed under-soil heating.

FRIDAY 29 DECEMBER 1995

Trained at Redcar again this afternoon. It's still very cold and today there was freezing fog to contend with as well. When we arrived at the beach we couldn't tell whether the tide was in or out, it was that bad. Fortunately, it was out and we got some training in. Travelled to Nottingham this afternoon.

It looks as if the gaffer will not be playing tomorrow. His calf is giving him a lot of problems. We're suffering from so many injuries at the moment, it's frightening. Jan Fjortoft pulled out this morning as well with a bad groin.

SATURDAY 30 DECEMBER 1995

Forest beat us 1-0 to give us our fourth away defeat on the trot. It was a much better performance all round considering our current situation regarding injuries and suspensions. John Hendrie, in particular, played very well. Clayton Blackmore made his first start of the season and I thought he played well. I was pleased for him because he is in a very similar situation to myself and it was nice to see him get back in the team. They scored early in the game with a Stuart Pearce penalty. I think it would have been very interesting if they hadn't scored so early because their crowd would have started getting on their back, and it would have worked in our favour.

There's a doubt about Monday's game against Villa. The pitch is still frozen. To be honest, because of our injuries and the fact that Villa have yet to play a game over the very busy Christmas period, it would probably be better for us if it was called off. We'll have to wait and see. There will be a pitch inspection at noon tomorrow.

SUNDAY 31 DECEMBER 1995

The game tomorrow is definitely on after a pitch inspection this morning, so no night out tonight to see in the New Year. Never mind.

Had a couple of drinks at Coxy's with Phil Whelan and our girlfriends but we were all tucked up in bed before 1.00 am.

MONDAY 1 JANUARY 1996

HAPPY NEW YEAR!!!

Let's hope 1996 will be as successful for the club as 1995. When you look back, and realise how far the club has come and achieved in one year, it's really amazing. Everybody at the club, from the manager and players to the office staff and laundry ladies, has played their part in turning the club's fortunes around - that and Steve Gibson's cheque book.

Unfortunately, the new year got off to a bad start with a 2-0 defeat at the hands of Aston Villa. You could tell which team had played three games in a week and which team hadn't. That, together with our growing injury crisis (add John Hendrie to the list - groin injury), put us on the road to another defeat.

The lads never gave up, but Villa scored two great goals in the first half and it was always going to be hard to pull it back. Villa looked very sharp and I was quite impressed with them.

Manchester United lost 4-1 at Spurs and it is a big blow to their title chances.

We have only one striker fit at the moment, Jaime Moreno, so Bob Ward will have his work cut out to get the lads fit for our FA Cup game at Notts County on Saturday.

TUESDAY 2 JANUARY 1996

All the lads who played yesterday are off until Thursday, but I trained at Ayresome Park with Phil Whelan and we're both down to play at York tomorrow night in the reserves.

Paul Wilkinson was in this morning and his loan period at Watford has finished. It might be a blessing in disguise because he will be available for the weekend if needed. But will the manager play him? I would.

WEDNESDAY 3 JANUARY 1996

Played in the reserves tonight and we drew 0-0. Phil Whelan had his first full game back after breaking his jaw. He played well considering it was his first game for nearly three months. I was quite surprised he lasted 90 minutes.

Paul Wilkinson also played and he really impressed me with his attitude and performance. It's never easy when you've played for the first team (on loan to Watford) and then gone straight back into the reserves, but he looked good. He is also one of the best defenders of set pieces I've ever known.

I came through the game OK and even though I didn't have a lot of saves to make, I was always involved and was quite satisfied with what I had to do. There was a situation in the game where a free-kick was taken and I made a very good finger-tip save to just push it around the post, but the referee didn't spot it and gave a goal-kick. Their players protested but he stood by his decision. It's funny sometimes because you want people to know you've made a good save, but you don't want to concede a corner. Can't win really, can you?

A few of the younger lads caught my eye with very good performances tonight. Alan White, Mickey Barron and especially the young Mickey Cummins, who I thought had an excellent game in midfield. He is definitely a name to look out for.

THURSDAY 4 JANUARY 1996

Went into training this morning even though all the other lads were off. I felt I needed a good session with Mike - and got one!

Jan Fjortoft pulled out of training again. It fuelled speculation that Wilko might play on Saturday. It would be an ideal game for him but we'll have to wait and see. If he doesn't play again now, he never will.

Played golf this afternoon. Maybe I shouldn't have on a Thursday, but the way things are at the moment, it's a kind of release for me and I'm sure it doesn't do me any harm. In fact I thoroughly enjoyed it and I felt quite refreshed afterwards. It was probably only because I got a birdie on the last because I was knackered really.

Had an hour at the greyhounds at Cleveland Park in the evening with Phil and Coxy just to pass some time. It's not the best dog track in the world but everybody is always friendly towards us and it's a good atmosphere. It is if our dog crosses the finish line first, anyway. Phil and myself were gutted because Coxy could have a drink tonight as he's suspended for the next two games. I'm sure he enjoyed drinking his lager in front of us while we had our cokes.

FRIDAY 5 JANUARY 1996

Paul Wilkinson trained this morning and afterwards he was told to go home and get his tracksuit and be prepared to travel. When I saw him training in the morning I thought he was being overlooked, but there was obviously a change of heart and he was included. Stayed at a hotel in the centre of Nottingham.

SATURDAY 6 JANUARY 1996

We beat Notts County 2-1 today. Any result in the FA Cup away from home is a good one and this was no exception. It was a real battle as well with County playing the long ball game. Wilko played and, considering the game we were playing, I thought it was a wise decision - he holds the ball up very well. I thought he played well and so did all the other lads. It was never going to be a classic, but all that matters is that we are in the next round. Nick Barmby and Jamie Pollock scored the goals very early in the second half. County got a goal back shortly afterwards, but we held out.

I went out in the evening with my girlfriend, Jo, Nigel Pearson and his wife, Nicky, and former Boro player Mark Proctor and his wife, Julie. It was Nicky's 30th birthday. We had a very nice evening, especially when Nigel paid. The only problem we had was when the coach dropped Nigel and me off on the A19. We had to run across the dual carriageway in pitch black. Not a good idea but we managed to make it.

MONDAY 8 JANUARY 1996

All the players trained today except Curtis Fleming who picked up another injury on Saturday and may now be out for two or three weeks. I think he must have run over a black cat! He's been so unlucky this season and he's such a hard working lad, I hope he gets back soon.

Played golf this afternoon with Coxy and then Nigel Pearson and Mike Kelly joined us. It was really windy and raining, we must be mad.

TUESDAY 9 JANUARY 1996

There was nearly a fight in training today between Nick Barmby and Jan Fjortoft. It had been building up for a couple of days, then there was a bad challenge and they both kept winding each other up. By the end of the session, they were nearly at each other's throats. It was more like handbags at half paces.

It might seem strange to say this but sometimes an argument like that can be good for team morale. It sort of clears the air. Whenever anything like this happens, the lads love it. We were winding them up even more and Nigel Pearson made a mock boxing ring in the dressing room for them when they had finished training. We all had a good laugh about it afterwards. These things are quickly forgotten.

During a season, when you are with people every day there are bound to be some disputes. There are people at the club from all different backgrounds, walks of life and countries so you get clashes. It happens at every club. Sometimes the tension and pressure gets on top of people and it shows you care when you get a reaction like that.

WEDNESDAY 10 JANUARY 1996

Played in the reserves against Burnley tonight and, unfortunately, we lost our first game at home, going down 2-1.

Jan played an hour and came through OK, as did Craig Hignett and Graham Kavanagh. Gordon was gutted after the game because we could have gone 12 points clear at the top of the table. We gave away two bad goals from corners and we had enough chances to win the game. I had to make a couple of good saves and, overall, I was pleased. Sometimes if you play well, you think that you're being wasted playing in the reserves and should be in the first team,

A Miller's Tale

where you would get more credit for your performance. On the other hand, if you play badly, you start doubting yourself because you can't even play well in the reserves.

Shock News!!!

Terry Venables has announced he's quitting the England job after the Euro 96 Championships. A few possible candidates have been announced including our gaffer, Bryan Robson, who is one of the favourites. It will be interesting to see the reaction tomorrow.

THURSDAY 11 JANUARY 1996

GIVE MY JOBBO TO ROBBO!!!

That's The Sun's headline this morning. I bet everyone on Teesside is in shock at the thought of him leaving Boro. I had a day off this morning so I wasn't there to see the reaction of the players, but my first thought was that it would be terrible to lose the gaffer now. It would really set us back after what we have achieved. - who could replace him? He must be tempted to go for it but he's still young in management terms and I think it might be too soon for him.

I saw Curtis Fleming at Springs and he told me that the manager had held a meeting with the players. He told them he had not been offered the job and he wasn't interested in it at the moment anyway. I think it was important he cleared the air straight away, that way he doesn't create any uncertainty at the club. I'm sure he will be offered the job in a few years' time anyway and he will relish the challenge and do well.

He also told the players we are going on a four day trip to Tenerife after the cup game against Watford or Wimbledon on 27 January. Much more important than the England manager's job, surely! I bet that will go down like a lead balloon with the wives and girlfriends.

FRIDAY 12 JANUARY 1996

A reporter and photographer from Esquire magazine were at training today. We must be going places. I made sure I got the bottom goal in the five-a-side so the photographer could get my best side!

I did an article for the club's Red Roar magazine this afternoon with my girlfriend, Jo. They took some pictures at home and then at Yarm 85. It seemed to go well but we'll have to wait and see the results.

I'm not involved tomorrow so I will be training in the morning with Mike Kelly. It's going to be so frustrating not playing against Arsenal, probably the worst feeling so far this season. I'll have to put a brave face on it. It will be good to see a few old faces.

SATURDAY 13 JANUARY 1996

Another defeat for us, 3-2 to my old club. We led 2-1 at one stage and were in a commanding position but we seem to have started conceding goals all of a sudden. Juninho scored again with Phil Stamp getting the other with a great goal.

Talking of Stampy, he had a great piece in the programme. In his player's profile he was asked which was the favourite hotel he'd ever stayed in. He replied: "The one in Nottingham, I can't remember the name". Stampy is a lovely, genuine lad but he comes out with some real crackers sometimes.

Had a drink with Malcolm Allison and Coxy in Yarm after the game and he told us a story about a young pro, years ago at Spurs when Bill Nicholson was manager. He had just bought his first car and was driving out of White Hart Lane into the busy High Road when he was hit by an oncoming bus and wrecked his car. He ran back to the ground and into Mr Nicholson's office asking what he should do. Bill Nicholson told him to calm down and then asked: "Did you get the number of the bus?" He replied: "Yes, it was a 67".

Had a meal in the evening with my brother and his girlfriend, Jo's aunt and Coxy and his girlfriend, Rachel. Had a great night, especially watching Coxy eat oysters for the first time. I bet Rachel had a good night!

MONDAY 15 JANUARY 1996

Forty new training balls have been stolen over the weekend from Ayresome Park. How they got past the 24-hour security guards, I'll never know. Apparently they stopped Mike Kelly when he was leaving the ground thinking he had a ball under his jumper but when they searched him they realised it was just over indulgence.

TUESDAY 16 JANUARY 1996

Played for the reserves again tonight against Bradford. The referee actually abandoned the game after 37 minutes because of thick fog. We were 3-1 up at the time. We were sitting in the dressing room contemplating the thought of having to go back again when the fog lifted.

Gordon McQueen asked the referee if we could go back out, their manager agreed and we played the rest of the game. It's very unusual for refs to use common sense and change their minds! Craig Hignett scored one and Jaime Moreno got the other two. We won 3-2 to maintain our lead at the top of the league.

THURSDAY 18 JANUARY 1996

We were told today that we're travelling to Southampton tomorrow by coach and it will take about six hours to get there because the club can't arrange any flights. It's going to be a nightmare because our coach is about as comfortable as a park bench! I must remember to pack pillows, blankets, books and videos. It's like going on manoeuvres.

Juninho pulled out of training today and is now a doubt for Saturday. Another big blow.

FRIDAY 19 JANUARY 1996

After the six hour coach journey it was a relief to eventually reach Southampton. Juninho hasn't travelled so we're now down to the bare bones. It will be interesting to see what the team will be tomorrow.

SATURDAY 20 JANUARY 1996

We were 1-0 up at half-time against Southampton and in a very good position. Gary Walsh made a very, very good save just before half time to keep us in the game.

In the second half, we held out quite well with Gary having to make another couple of very good saves. Then Phil Whelan got booked and Southampton scored from the resulting free-kick.

Unfortunately, Phil got his second booking and was sent off in the 70th minute. They again scored from the free kick and so Phil was ultimately blamed for the loss of the game. We've now lost five on the trot. We need to get a result soon but we have been torn apart by injuries. I felt sorry for Phil on the way home because I know how much of a livewire he is, I could tell he was genuinely gutted. He looked very low.

I have felt quite good lately but after the game today I felt very low myself and that nagging feeling came back that I'm too good to be sitting about not playing. It's a very desperate situation to be in. Before today, I had come to terms with it but, after feeling so good in training, I again feel like I should be playing and making a name for myself. Only time will tell.

We eventually got back to Teesside at about 11pm. It was the first time I've seen Match of the Day for a long time.

MONDAY 22 JANUARY 1996

Played golf with Phil Whelan after training and beat him on the 18th with a 6ft putt. He was gutted.

The gaffer is away with the England squad, as is Nick Barmby and Mike Kelly, so it's just the sick, the lame and the lazy training at the moment.

TUESDAY 23 JANUARY 1996

Enjoyed training today. We played various small sided games, head tennis, five-a-side, relay races and ended it with a Tug of War. My team won easily. It made a nice change. We are always training very hard every day so it was good to have a more light-hearted session, especially considering the injuries we have and no game again until the weekend.

It's reported that Newcastle are trying to sign Asprilla from Parma for £6.7 million. It's another sign that big name stars are interested in coming to England to play. It's very encouraging.

WEDNESDAY 24 JANUARY 1996

Played in the reserves tonight and we beat Coventry 5-0 to go nine points clear of them, with a game in hand. Gordon McQueen was delighted. Chris Freestone scored another hat-trick. I wonder if he'll get his first team chance between now and the end of the season.

THURSDAY 25 JANUARY 1996

Mike Kelly was back today so Gary and myself had a good session (training session that is, he's not my type!) and enjoyed it. We all had to go back to the Cellnet Riverside Stadium today for a signing session of footballs and shirts for charity. Coxy and myself then went to a local school with club mascot Roary the Lion and PC Peacock to tell the kids to behave well and always tell their parents where they are going. It's a funny thing but Roary the Lion is supposed to be a mascot, especially for the children, yet whenever I've been to schools with him there's always a couple of them who burst out crying and are scared to death of him. Or is it me and Coxy?

FRIDAY 26 JANUARY 1996

We had a couple of inches of snow overnight and it's drifting this morning in strong winds. We just managed to train but the conditions were getting worse all the time. Juninho is definitely out tomorrow, as is Phil Stamp, the gaffer, Robbie Mustoe, Jamie Pollock and Graham Kavanagh. Derek Whyte passed a fitness test.

Juninho's English is getting slightly better, or is it his sense of humour. He took the Mickey out of Clayton's silver spaceman jacket when it was hanging up by his place. They obviously don't have them in Brazil, for obvious reasons.

SATURDAY 27 JANUARY 1996

The FA Cup game against Wimbledon today was called off. It snowed very heavily overnight and was still drifting a lot in the wind. It will probably do us a favour to get a few more people fit for the rearranged game. I hope it stops snowing soon. We're supposed to fly to Tenerife in the morning.

SUNDAY 28 JANUARY 1996

No more snow overnight so the trip was on. We all arrived at Teesside Airport at 6.45am for the start of a 13½ hour trip. It included three flights - to Heathrow where we had to wait two-and-a-half hours to get a flight to Madrid, then there was another two hour wait to get a flight to Tenerife. It was alright on the way there but it's going to be a nightmare on the way back. The gaffer and John Pickering didn't come along. They've gone off to Italy to look at a couple of players.

The lads preparing for a tough day out on the golf course during the Tenerife trip. Who says footballers don't work hard!

We eventually arrived at Tenerife and our hotel at 8.00pm. We met in the hotel bar at 9.00pm and then went out. At this time in Tenerife it's dead and we realised after tonight it's not worth going out until about 11.30pm. Unfortunately, because of all the travelling, by then we were all a little worse for wear. Nothing to do with the San Miguel!

MONDAY 29 JANUARY 1996

No training today. We all met for breakfast at a bar over the road from our hotel for a local dish - 16 full English breakfasts and a mug of tea. There was no sign of any sun so most of the lads decided to play golf. I played with Gary Walsh, Phil Whelan and Jaime Moreno. Phil won the money. After a few drinks at the golf club, we returned for a shower at the hotel. We all met up across the road again. The entertainment was a transvestite comedian called Crystal Starr - very funny. Later on in the evening, he/she dragged Viv Anderson up on stage. Viv told her/him his name was David and he was a dustman. He got absolutely hammered off the lads and, unfortunately for him, he was caught on camera. We all had a good night.

TUESDAY 30 JANUARY 1996

Trained at 10.00 am at a local stadium. It rained today, still no sign of the sun - just as well as there were a few weary eyes this morning.

Played golf again this afternoon against Phil. He won again. He obviously plays better in the warmer climate because he's never beaten me in England. I'll have to remember that in the summer. We came off the course early because it was absolutely bucketing down.

As soon as we returned, we got news of the afternoon's events for the non-golfers. Jamie Pollock and John Hendrie supposedly had an England v Scotland drinking contest. Unfortunately for John, he didn't realise Jamie was throwing most of his away. Derek Whyte kept winding him up by singing Flower of Scotland while the England contingent was singing Swing Low Sweet Chariot! Three-quarters of the way through, John apparently was saying to Jamie: "I'm a man, you're just a boy" and "Get your kids on the table".

Eventually, they went on to Sangria and, after the third jug, John crashed out and was carried home to bed. It was a very silly thing to do on a club trip with 19 other players. Consequently, one of his eyebrows somehow vanished!

We took him upstairs and made sure he was lying in the right position then we started to think what we could do. It was actually Jaime Moreno who got hold of Curtis Fleming's beard trimmer and Jaime shaved half his eyebrow off. He also shaved a patch out of the back of his head and wrote "666" on it. We were rolling around laughing.

We met some Wigan Rugby League players tonight, including Shaun Edwards. I thought we drank a lot when we went out, but that lot are professionals. I think we had better keep John away from them. He'll be challenging them next. He would probably lose more than a leg though, and he'd struggle to get any more kids on the table!

WEDNESDAY 31 JANUARY 1996

I've never seen anything as funny in all my life as when John came down for breakfast this morning. He had shaved the other eyebrow off as well and he looked like he was wearing a wig.

He hadn't even noticed the patch on the back of his head and we couldn't believe our luck when John was picked to go topless for the "skins" team against the "shirts" in training - we had also written "Help me!" on his back with a marker pen. None of us could stand up we were laughing so much. John didn't have a clue what was going on.

We had the first sunny day today so I spent some time around the pool with Derek, John, Phil, Jan and Viv. We had a meal organised in the evening but, just before that, Viv had to do an interview with Tenerife TV with us mingling in the background. One of the lads bought a condom from the toilet and Neil Cox casually placed it on Viv's shoulder while he was being interviewed by the female presenter. She didn't know where to look. Unfortunately, it fell off half-way through the interview.

On the way back from the meal, our kit man Tommy Johnson gave us a few songs. I think he must have had a few sangrias. We went to the local bar again to be entertained by Crystal. We got Mike Kelly drunk and by the end of the night he was dancing, although he couldn't remember it the next morning.

THURSDAY 1 FEBRUARY 1996

I take back what I said about the funniest thing I've ever seen. John Hendrie came down this morning with a red swollen face after his day in the sun yesterday and, with no eyebrows, he was the spitting image of Nicki Lauda. God knows what his wife is going to say. She might not recognise him. If he plays on Sunday the fans will probably shout for Nicki Lauda on the wing.

It was a long journey home with a delay at Heathrow for good measure. We left the hotel at 9.00 am and eventually arrived home at 11.00pm. I now feel how John looks, so I'm glad to get to bed.

FRIDAY 2 FEBRUARY 1996

Trained at 11.00am and had a good hard session. "Play hard, work hard", as Viv said while we were away when he was making the lads run around the pitch. I wouldn't mind, but he was always the last one in.

A Miller's Tale

SATURDAY 3 FEBRUARY 1996

Back to the serious stuff today as we prepare for Sunday's game at Chelsea. We have still got so many injuries, it's frightening. At least Robbie Mustoe returned to light training and it's good to see him getting back - he's an important player for us. We've only got two recognised midfield players fit - Clayton Blackmore and Craig Hignett, who has only just recovered from a hernia operation.

SUNDAY 4 FEBRUARY 1996

Chelsea stuffed us 5-0. It was our worst result and performance of the season. We were really poor. I thought before the game that if we could get any kind of result it would be tremendous. I think you have to look at the situation regarding injuries and suspensions at the moment. It's not an excuse, but our midfield today was Keith O'Halloran, Craig Liddle and Clayton Blackmore. I rate Keith and Craig very highly, and they've got great futures, but they are far more comfortable in defence where they normally play. That's no disrespect to them, but they would probably say the same, so it's evidence of how bad the injuries are at the moment. If it doesn't change soon, the gaffer is going to have to get the cheque book out again. I think the gaffer thought he would have two or three other players fit for today's game, but unfortunately they didn't quite make it.

After the game, Mike Kelly and Alan Hudson, who's working for Chelsea, had an argument in the tunnel and it got very heated. They had to be pulled apart. Apparently, Mike failed Hudson when he took an FA coaching course a few years ago and consequently Hudson had a go at Mike in a magazine. Mike had been biding his time to pull him up on it and he did just that.

Neil Cox had a bad day all round. Yesterday, while he was asleep, his living room ceiling collapsed because of a leaking pipe. Still, I suppose it could have been worse - he could have been sitting underneath it.

MONDAY 5 FEBRUARY 1996

The papers have picked up on the incident in the tunnel after the game and are making quite a thing of it. Mike could do without the bad publicity because he is employed by the FA as England's goalkeeping coach.

There's more snow forecast for this week but hopefully it won't disrupt our game on Wednesday night against Wimbledon. I played in the reserves at Hull and, would you believe it, it suddenly became very windy. We won 3-0, continuing our good run, but it was bloody freezing.

I saw a funny thing after the game. John Hendrie knew one of their players and was going to have a quick drink with him after the game. After having a shower, he went up to the mirror to do his hair. Well, that's what I thought, but on looking again, I saw he was touching up his eyebrows with an eyeliner pencil. I've seen it all now!

TUESDAY 6 FEBRUARY 1996

The Brazilian Branco was introduced to all the players this morning and trained with us at a local prison. We had to use the Astroturf there because the pitch was frozen at Ayresome. I don't think he could quite believe the writing on the wall in the dressing room. If he signs, I'm sure it won't be long before he's up there somewhere.

A Miller's Tale

A collection of Nigel Pearson's dressing room drawings on the wall at Ayresome Park. John Collins is the guy with the quiff, drawn when we thought he was going to sign. Pay Cut's Place refers to Craig Hignett's decision to stay with the club rather than leave on a free and the fat goalie is Nigel's generous analysis of my training efforts.

Nigel's contribution to my place in the dressing room followed an incident when I snapped at Mike Kelly. I missed a shot in training and he had a go. I said "I'm trying my best. I'm working hard honest". The next day there was a picture of a fat goalkeeper sitting on a ball with those words in a speech bubble.

Branco hasn't signed yet and went back to the Riverside after training to sort out personal terms of his contract. I'd love to be a fly on the wall. Players never really talk about what money they are on but I'm sure Branco will do pretty well.

There isn't too much resentment about players earning a lot more money, good luck to them, but I think it's unfair when new players come in on enormous wages and those who have been here a while and worked hard get told there's a wage structure when they go to negotiate new contracts. That doesn't do much for team morale.

Jamie Pollock looks as if he'll be fit for tomorrow but Juninho is still a doubt. Jan Fjortoft is away on international duty, so Paul Wilkinson will play up front.

WEDNESDAY 7 FEBRUARY 1996

A goal-less draw with Wimbledon tonight in the FA Cup at the Riverside. We never really looked like scoring and it was a disappointing game.

The crowd seemed very restless, which is understandable after our recent run of results, but it didn't really help the cause. Juninho was passed fit before the game and played well in patches. Jamie Pollock played well on his return, as did Paul Wilkinson. The replay is next Tuesday.

A Miller's Tale

Spoke to Sunderland manager Peter Reid after the game and he said he needed £2 million and he felt he would get them promotion. He really fancies getting Niall Quinn to lead the attack, but he doubts whether the board will give him any more money. It makes you realise how much Steve Gibson has pumped into our club, not only for players, but also for a brand new stadium. You have to admire his ambition.

THURSDAY 8 FEBRUARY 1996

Branco has finally signed for us, for 18 months. He's a free agent so he'll cost the club nothing. Sounds a good bit of business but I'm sure he'll make it up in wages. The club must wait for a work permit before he can play and, apparently, it will take three or four weeks. I'm not sure if he'll relish the weather. Today, everywhere was frozen so we were running on the beach at Redcar. Lovely!

FRIDAY 9 FEBRUARY 1996

Struggled to find a place to train this morning. Some trained in the gym, the rest at a local park - not ideal preparation for the big match tomorrow against Newcastle. I'm sure they must be in the same boat though.

Jo and I went to a museum which was showing an exhibition on Ayresome Park and especially the last year there. It was very interesting and there were quite a few pictures I was in. It makes you realise that I was involved in something very special and an important part of the club's history. There were some amazing paintings as well.

SATURDAY 10 FEBRUARY 1996

Middlesbrough 1 Newcastle 2. I can't really believe we lost this game. We were the better side. We were 1-0 up at half time and deservedly so, even though it was an own goal by John Beresford. Gary Walsh made a couple of very good saves but other than that we had most of the play. It was played in an electric atmosphere. We were still on top until 20 minutes from the end when Keegan brought Asprilla on for his debut. At first, he looked very clumsy and lazy but it took him only a few minutes to make an impact. He turned Steve Vickers inside out before delivering a perfect cross for Watson to head home.

I thought at that stage it would have been a slightly disappointing result but then they scored the winner through Les Ferdinand. He shot from just outside the box and somehow it seemed to go under the body of Gary Walsh. I'm sure Walshy was devastated he let the ball go under his body. I felt sorry for him because it's easily done, but, unfortunately, it was the winner in a North East derby. I found it hard after the game because I wanted to say "unlucky" to him, but I'm sure he would have thought I was being sarcastic.

It's a very difficult situation because I want us to win but, at the end of the day, I want to be playing again. I don't want Gary to make mistakes but I suppose the only way I will play is if he does. I'm sure he would think the same! There's never been any animosity between me and Gary but both of us want to play.

We don't socialise but that's not because we don't get on, it's mostly because he has got a wife and family. We are different characters, he's got a more settled life and I have more free time on my hands. But we spend a lot of time together in training along with Ben Roberts and have a good laugh. I obviously think I'm a better keeper, you've got to have confidence in your own ability, but I'm sure he does the same and Ben thinks he's better than both of us.

MONDAY 12 FEBRUARY 1996

Trained this afternoon at Ayresome, then flew down to London for our game against Wimbledon tomorrow night. I decided to run a book on the cricket World Cup. I had the fright of my life when the gaffer said he would have £500 on South Africa at 6/1, so I quickly said it had to be cash up front. Luckily he only had £50 on him.

The prices were:

Australia	3/1
Pakistan	4/1
India	5/1
South Africa	6/1
West Indies	6/1
England	9/1
Sri Lanka	12/1
New Zealand	30/1
Others	250/1

There was a lot of interest at the dinner table and most of the money went on the West Indies and South Africa. I'll be in a bit of trouble if either of them win. Only £20 was put on England so there's not a lot of confidence there, but I'll be laughing if Sri Lanka win.

TUESDAY 13 FEBRUARY 1996

It was the replay against Wimbledon tonight. We lost another disappointing game, 1-0, and we're now out of both cups. It's a blow to realise you're not going to win anything. We thought we had a good chance to get to a big final but we just can't seem to win a game, or even draw lately.

We played OK in the first half and had three great chances, but, yet again, we failed to score. After 15 minutes of the second half, the game became very scrappy, which is just what they wanted, and Dean Holdsworth scored 15 minutes from time. Nick Barmby had a great chance right at the end, but his shot hit the crossbar and that summed up our night. The players were really low after the game.

WEDNESDAY 14 FEBRUARY 1996

After travelling back from London, Jan, Alan Moore, Clayton and myself had to meet up at Ayresome Park and travel to Burnley for a reserve game. It feels like I've been from one end of the country to the other. Derek Whyte, Curtis Fleming and Robbie Mustoe made their comebacks and all come through the game very well. We won 3-0.

After the game, we were invited into the vice-president's lounge where the bar was open and they laid on pie and peas. I've started to get a taste for this.

THURSDAY 15 FEBRUARY 1996

Alan Smith and his family have come up to visit us for a few days. It's good to see him. We managed to get out on to a nearby golf course today and we were having a good round until I spotted Mike Kelly on the first tee. As it was Thursday, I wasn't supposed to be playing. I ended up playing only two more holes hiding behind hedges and in bunkers. The other players must have thought I was mad. Smudge is currently working for "Four Four Two" magazine on a regular basis and also for various newspapers.

FRIDAY 16 FEBRUARY 1996

After training, I went to the pictures and then to Yarm 85 restaurant. I'm not involved again tomorrow, surprise surprise! I've decided not to train in the morning and to train on Sunday instead simply because Smudge has to leave tomorrow morning. It'll give me more time to spend with him.

Mike didn't mention the golf so I think I might have got away with it. No Juninho tomorrow, he's away with Brazil.

SATURDAY 17 FEBRUARY 1996

A disastrous result today - a 4-1 home defeat to bottom-of-the-table Bolton. If we're not careful, we're going to get ourselves in trouble. We keep shooting ourselves in the foot. Bolton didn't even play particularly well and still scored four goals. We've lost eight league games on the trot and let in 23 goals in the process. The gaffer had a real go after the game and said it looked as if we were waiting for a 39-year-old man to come in and sort it all out for us. He was very disappointed. We must turn this around soon, otherwise, we could be in trouble. We've had a lot of injuries and suspensions, but we're now starting to get people back and we need a win. West Ham and QPR, two of the teams close to us, both won which hasn't helped us.

SUNDAY 18 FEBRUARY 1996

After the last few weeks, and the way things have gone, I genuinely feel that I am worthy of a recall. No disrespect to Gary, but sometimes when things are not going too well, it's worth a change. I've kept working hard and would love another crack in the team. I really would love to play on Saturday against Coventry, but, unfortunately, it's not down to me.

Trained this morning with Mike because we've got a reserve game tomorrow against Aston Villa. It will be the first one at the Riverside Stadium. I don't think the gaffer is ready to play, but Viv Anderson is, which is interesting as Nigel Pearson is suspended on Saturday.

MONDAY 19 FEBRUARY 1996

The reserve game tonight still went ahead despite appalling conditions - it was a virtual blizzard. The Forest v Spurs game tonight was abandoned after 15 minutes. We won the game 2-1 and strengthened our position in the Pontin's League still further. John Hendrie and Graham Kavanagh scored our goals. Viv came through unscathed.

TUESDAY 20 FEBRUARY 1996

The pitch at Ayresome was frozen today so we did some running around it instead of training. Had a word with the gaffer after training about my situation. He said he felt it would be harsh on Walshy if he dropped him now and said he felt only one goal was his fault. I said I disagreed and felt that if I wasn't going to get in the team now, I never would. He said he could appreciate my position and he would be looking at it closely. I wasn't blaming Walshy or having a go at him personally to the gaffer, just summing up the current situation we're in.

It obviously means I won't be playing on Saturday and left me feeling very negative as I was gearing myself up to be playing. Had a drink in Yarm this evening and popped into the casino in Middlesbrough. I put it all on black and it came up red. Just my luck!

WEDNESDAY 21 FEBRUARY 1996

The club is struggling to get Branco a work permit in time for Saturday's game. Some reports say we might struggle to get one at all because he hasn't played for Brazil in the last year. The club is arguing that Brazil have been preparing for the Olympics where there is an age restriction of 23, and 23 Branco isn't!

THURSDAY 22 FEBRUARY 1996

I felt rough this morning and didn't go into training. I think I must have picked up a bug that's been going around the club. I'm hoping to be OK to travel to Coventry tomorrow.

FRIDAY 23 FEBRUARY 1996

Had a very rough night last night and there's no way I'll be able to travel today. So, after ringing Bob Ward, it was back to bed. Didn't feel any better all day.

SATURDAY 24 FEBRUARY 1996

We picked up a point with a goal-less draw at Coventry and, at last, we've stopped the rot with an important away point. It was very strange today, not being at the game and listening to it on the radio. It sounded like a very hard-working performance and a well-deserved draw. There didn't seem to be many chances, but, by all accounts, Jan had the best one in the first half, which Ogrizovic did well to save. Robbie Mustoe, Graham Kavanagh and Curtis Fleming all made very good comebacks and I was pleased to hear that Phil Whelan got man of the match from Century Radio. Let's hope this result will put our bad run behind us and we can start winning again.

SUNDAY 25 FEBRUARY 1996

Felt really rough again today and was sick when I tried to eat this afternoon. I'm hoping to see the doctor tomorrow. I don't think I'll be training very much this week if this keeps up.

Leeds beat Birmingham and reached the Coca-Cola Cup Final. They will play against Villa on 24 March. I bet it will be a very good game and my money is on Villa.

MONDAY 26 FEBRUARY 1996

I saw the club doctor, Dr Dunn, this afternoon and he told me I've got some sort of stomach bug. I will have to have just fluids and no solid foods of any kind for three days to let the tablets work which he has given me. Unfortunately, no alcoholic fluids allowed!

Branco's work permit has been issued and he can now play for us. I think he's an important addition to our squad, especially at a time when it's all hands to the pumps. I'm not sure if he'll play on Saturday, but I'm sure he'll be involved in some respect.

TUESDAY 27 FEBRUARY 1996

Spoke to the former Arsenal goalkeeper and TV presenter Bob Wilson on the phone today. It was good to speak to him about my current situation and dealing with the frustration. It meant a lot to me for him to ring. He took the time to speak to me even though his daughter is seriously ill with cancer. I've got so much time for him. He's been a big influence on my career, but, apart from that, he's a genuinely lovely bloke.

I met Bob when I was a young kid at Arsenal and he coached me for eight years, he was brilliant. In my first year, I found it very hard and he was a big help. In the second year I really came on and got a contract. He always said to me that sometimes everything goes well and you're on a roll and then suddenly it all goes against you. He used to look at the clock and think "five minutes and I haven't let a goal in" and get through a game like that. I always remember that and try to be positive. With a legend like Bob, you would think he never had a bad game but it has been good advice.

WEDNESDAY 28 FEBRUARY 1996

God knows how Phil Whelan coped when he had his jaw wired up for six months, I'm struggling after two days. I spoke to Phil this afternoon and he loved the fact that I couldn't eat for a few days because we all gave him so much stick when he couldn't eat. I think he was getting his own back. I'm hoping to get back to training on Friday and maybe do a little light running. Some might say that's all I do anyway.

I must admit I'm missing the banter of the dressing room already. It has a contagious effect on you and I'm sure a lot of footballers, when they've finished playing, must miss that side of it nearly as much as playing. Let's hope that's a long way off.

THURSDAY 29 FEBRUARY 1996

Vince O'Keefe from the PFA came to see me this morning to talk to be about my pension and contributions. A footballer can obtain his pension at 35 years of age, so it's very important to fund this as much as you can while you're playing so you can reap the benefits later.

It made me realise that, however much you enjoy playing the game, at the end of the day, it's really all about securing your future by using wisely the money you earn. All too often, players earn fortunes and blow it all. Then, all of a sudden, they finish, the money dries up and they are left with nothing. I don't want to end up like that.

FRIDAY 1 MARCH 1996

Went back to training today and managed a few laps jogging round the pitch and, afterwards, a few light weights. I felt fairly weak, to be honest, which, I suppose, is understandable. It was good to be in the dressing room again and, even though I've been away just over a week, there's already a couple of new drawings on the walls.

It looks as if Mickey Barron will play tomorrow as Nigel Pearson and Phil Whelan are suspended and Steve Vickers failed a fitness test today. Even though Mickey has only made a couple of first team appearances, I'm sure he'll do OK, after playing with him on numerous occasions in the reserves.

After beating Phil Whelan at golf - he definitely is a fair weather player - we decided to have a night out. We started off in Yarm where we bumped into Peter Reid again. He still can't get any money for players. Everything was going well until we went to Club M near Yarm, when Phil was chatted up by a 6ft transvestite. She said to him: "You're a big lad, are you in the forces?" On that note, we both moved on to another bar. I tell you what though, he/she had a great pair of legs!

SATURDAY 2 MARCH 1996

Another defeat today - 2-0 to Everton. For the first 20 minutes I thought we played really well and created some great chances, but, not for the first time this season, we couldn't convert any of them.

Gary Walsh had already made one excellent save when he tipped a shot onto the post only to see the rebound go straight to an Everton player, who duly scored. They scored their second through a penalty when Kanchelskis was brought down by Curtis Fleming, but, seeing it afterwards, Flem didn't touch him. Mind you, in the second half he did bring someone down and it wasn't given. Luckily enough for us, none of the other teams below won. Branco also made his debut as a late substitute and very nearly scored.

Went out in the evening to the Tontine for Derek Whyte's wife's (Wilma) and Paul Wilkinson's wife's (Sue) 30th birthdays. There were around 20 of us and it was a great night. After our meal, Wilma suggested that every 10 minutes the girls should move two seats around the massive table. I wasn't too sure about this at first but it turned out to be a great idea, getting to meet everyone. The only trouble was that you had the same conversation seven or eight times. After that, everybody took a turn to sing any kind of song. All finished off with a nice glass of vintage port. Lovely!

SUNDAY 3 MARCH 1996

I went to Springs this afternoon. It was supposed to be this morning but I had one too many ports last night. Had some lunch in Yarm where we met Neil Cox and Rachel. Liverpool beat Villa 3-0 today and can't be ruled out of the title race yet.

MONDAY 4 MARCH 1996

Trained properly with Mike Kelly today and knew about it. I was breathing very heavily and it wasn't always out of my mouth. It was important to get a good session under my belt.

Man United beat Newcastle tonight which completely throws open the title race. Newcastle dominated the first half and, but for

Schmeichel, could have been three or four up. Cantona scored for United in the second half.

TUESDAY 5 MARCH 1996

Trained hard again today, but still fell a little bit short of fitness. I'm going to play in tomorrow night's reserve game. I'm not sure whether I'll play 90 minutes. I could have done with another couple of day's more training, to be honest. Branco will definitely play which I'm sure will bring a big crowd to the Riverside.

Tommy Johnson, our kit man, came into the dressing room after training with a magnum of champagne and loads of birthday cake. It was his 70th birthday. I tell you what, he doesn't half look well on it. I hope I look as good as him when I'm 70. Thinking about it, I hope I look as good as him when I'm 50!

WEDNESDAY 6 MARCH 1996

Over 15,000 turned up at the Riverside tonight to watch the reserve game - or Branco really. They even had to put back the kick-off time by 15 minutes.

Unfortunately, we were rubbish and lost 2-0 to Leicester City, one of only three defeats this season. We've played some really good stuff this season, but, unfortunately, not tonight. It was really disappointing, not only for the fans, but for us as we all know what we've been playing like. I was disappointed with their second goal for which I blamed myself. I definitely needed the game after being out for a while.

Branco was fairly quiet, apart from some great corners and a couple of free kicks, one of which was about 50 yards out. At the end I thought he was going to try his luck from our goal kicks. I'm sure he would be livelier in a first team game.

Both Queens Park Rangers and Sheffield Wednesday lost again which can only help our cause. I bet we only need to win one more game to be safe.

THURSDAY 7 MARCH 1996

The gaffer has been away all week and nobody has really explained where he is. It's all very secretive. It must be important as our current situation is hardly ideal.

We all had a meeting this afternoon with John Knox who is the new marketing manager at the club. He was very efficient and seemed to have a lot of good ideas. While he was talking I had the idea of maybe seeing if anyone would be interested in publishing this diary. At first, I started it just for my own personal reference. One of the lads kept one while I was at Lilleshall and I thought it would be interesting to look back at in years to come. But, after realising just how much it has covered over the past few months, I thought it might be of interest to quite a few people. So if you are reading this, you must have bought a copy!

FRIDAY 8 MARCH 1996

Apart from Steve Vickers (injured), Phil Whelan and Jamie Pollock (both suspended), we've got a full squad to choose from tomorrow. It's the first time for ages we've had that luxury. It's an important game for us against West Ham. We're flying down to London in the morning.

SATURDAY 9 MARCH 1996

West Ham beat us 2-0. We're really not giving ourselves a chance at the moment. First, Gary Walsh made a mistake with a back pass after just 40 seconds and we went 1-0 down. Then, despite playing fairly well, especially after the break, we failed to create any really good goal-scoring opportunities. It seems that when we're away from home and go behind, we struggle to get anything from the game. We've only scored six away goals and two of them have been penalties, that's nowhere near enough. The two Brazilians went on as substitutes in the second half, but, at that stage, we were 2-0 down. The second goal was a penalty against Neil Cox, which was very dubious. The referee was the only person in the ground who thought it was. When things are going against you, these things happen.

Stayed down in London and went out with Alan Smith, Steve Bould and their wives.

SUNDAY 10 MARCH 1996

Had a drink with my dad today and saw a few old friends, then went back to my mum's for dinner. It seems a long time since I've done that.

MONDAY 11 MARCH 1996

Freezing cold today (again). We trained at Ayresome Park but there was no Mike Kelly so Gary and myself played out on pitch. All goalkeepers are frustrated centre-forwards anyway.

After training Phil Whelan, Neil Cox and myself played golf. Coxy won the money on the last hole after Phil hit his tee-shot all of six yards. I was already out of the equation (again!).

TUESDAY 12 MARCH 1996

Had a really crap day today. The less said the better, I think.

WEDNESDAY 13 MARCH 1996

I played in the reserves tonight and we beat York 4-0 to extend our lead even further. Branco played and looked a lot livelier than in his first game. He made two of our goals with great crosses and nearly scored himself straight from a corner. To be honest, every time we had a corner, we looked like scoring. I wonder if this will make the manager play him on Saturday, especially as we're not scoring at all at the moment.

Phil Whelan, Phil Stamp, Chris Freestone and Mickey Barron scored the goals. Another great crowd saw the game - 4,600 people turned up. At least this time they saw a few goals and a better performance.

THURSDAY 14 MARCH 1996

All the lads were buzzing when I walked into the dressing room. It didn't take me long to realise why. The West Indies were playing Australia today and most of them, including the gaffer, had placed a few quid on the Windies with me. They couldn't wait to tell me that the Aussies were currently 15 for 3. I tried to play it down but they knew I was desperate for Australia to win.

Gary's a good keeper and a nice lad. There's never been any bad feeling between us but, by the time March came around, I thought things were going badly enough for him and the team for me to deserve a recall. Unfortunately, it wasn't to be.

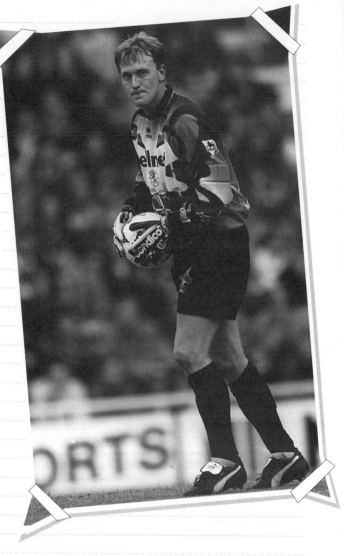

Later on, the Aussies rallied to get 204-7 and jut when the Windies looked like they were cruising to victory they collapsed and lost in the last over. I couldn't believe my luck - can't wait for training tomorrow. Sri Lanka have also made the final and nobody backed them so hopefully they can win.

FRIDAY 15 MARCH 1996

We've got a full squad to pick from tomorrow, barring Steve Vickers, so it'll be interesting what the team will be and whether Branco will play. Phil Whelan and Clayton Blackmore are both definitely not involved and will be training with the reserves tomorrow morning. To say they were unhappy is an understatement.

SATURDAY 16 MARCH 1996

I spoke to the gaffer again today before the game with Forest. I told him I wasn't happy because I thought I might have had a chance of playing. We've been on a bad run and, especially after the West Ham defeat, I thought if I didn't play now I never would. I don't want to have a go at Gary because we all make mistakes, but he made a bad one in that game and things aren't going well for the team. I felt after that, maybe I deserved a chance.

I told the manager I was feeling low and went through the games with him. I was in there for about 25 minutes. He was trying to reassure me but it's March now and I haven't played for months. I feel like I'm hitting my head against a brick wall. A lot was said and it seemed to clear the air a bit, but for how long? How many more times have I got to go and see him?

We drew the game with Forest which means another welcome point. With Coventry, Wimbledon and Southampton all losing, it's pulled us away a bit more from the bottom. Robbie Mustoe scored our goal to cap a very impressive performance from him. We got our goal straight after Forest, who scored on a break-away. Not a bad game or performance, but nothing inspiring.

Graham Kavanagh was dropped, along with Chris Morris and Craig Hignett. Kav took it very hard, which is understandable as he's played well since returning to the side. Branco, Juninho and Jamie Pollock returned.

SUNDAY 16 MARCH 1996

Trained with Ben Roberts and Mike Kelly at Ayresome Park today. Ben looked knackered after staying up all night with his mates to watch the Bruno v Tyson fight. It didn't start until 5.00 am and then lasted only three rounds with Tyson winning easily. I'm glad I didn't wait up now.

Sunderland won 2-0 at Birmingham and really look a good bet for promotion. It would be great to have three North East teams in the Premiership.

Sri Lanka have done it. They beat Australia easily to win the cricket World Cup and me £390. Not one single person had backed them. Maybe my luck is changing. Viv will be gutted.

MONDAY 17 MARCH 1996

After training, we travelled to Birmingham for our game tomorrow at Aston Villa. It wasn't the best of journeys as we must have the most uncomfortable coach of any football team.

The club took us to an Italian restaurant this evening for a meal which was nice. The gaffer and Viv met us there. Viv called me a lucky b*****d after my cricket success and I thanked him for his generosity.

TUESDAY 19 MARCH 1996

Uwe Fuchs came to our hotel today and came up to mine and Nigel Pearson's room for a chat in the afternoon. He's had an up and down time at Millwall and things haven't gone the way he was expecting.

There was a funny piece in the paper at the weekend about him. Jimmy Nicholl, his manager, was saying he wasn't happy with Millwall's performance in the first half against Sheffield United, so at half time he gave his side a roasting. He said Uwe took the brunt of his criticism and then, in the second half, he scored and they won 1-0. Nicholl said in the paper that he will have a go at Uwe at half-time every week if that's the result it gets. Unfortunately, the reporters must have spoken to Uwe shortly afterwards and when asked about it he replied: "I knew he was angry, but he talks too fast and I didn't understand a word he said". I bet the reporters loved him.

The lads drew 0-0 with Villa. The game never really got going. They had a few out, obviously because of their Cup Final on Sunday. It was a good chance for us to get a very good result but if you had said we would get a point beforehand, I think we would have taken it.

We didn't get back to Teesside until 1.45 am. GOODNIGHT!

WEDNESDAY 20 MARCH 1996

Graham Kavanagh is on the front page of the local paper for punching someone in the face on Saturday night. He was arrested but later released. Apparently, the lad was having a go at Alan Moore and Kav had had enough. The gaffer wasn't best pleased and pulled Kav in and told him he has to learn to turn the other cheek. I think he's learnt his lesson because it's very embarrassing for him, his family and the club.

Kav was told by the manager on Saturday that he was being left out. When he returned to the meeting room, you could tell he was very upset. The funny thing was, or not as the case may be, jokingly I said: "I bet you'll be fighting tonight Kav". Famous last words!

Kav obviously took it to heart when the manager left him out and he was still angry that night. He's quite an emotional lad. You can get people having a pop at you when they've had a few drinks and they obviously caught him at a bad time.

THURSDAY 21 MARCH 1996

Trained this morning and we had friendly match against local side Billingham Synthonia tonight. Most of us were down to play half a game each, except Branco who had to play the whole game - he was delighted, of course.

After the first half, we were only 1-0 up, but eventually won 7-1. I'm not sure if the team were a lot better in the second half or whether Synthonia got very tired.

We've got no game at the weekend as Villa are in the Cup Final so we've been told we're going to have the weekend off. Coxy and myself are going to London tomorrow after training and will return on Monday morning. It will be only the second time since early December I've been home and, as it's my birthday next week, it's worked out quite well.

FRIDAY 22 MARCH 1996

After training, it was a quick change and then a dash to Darlington station to catch the train. We just managed to get the 1.05pm train so we were hoping to miss the worst of the rush hour traffic when we got there.

We didn't quite manage it though, we just caught the beginning of it, but after living in the North East for 18 months, I had forgotten about traffic jams and it seemed like a lifetime.

We eventually arrived at the Swallow Hotel where we're staying and, after a cup of tea, it was time to get our dancing gear on. Manchester City are also staying in the hotel for their game at West Ham tomorrow and, as we left, we saw Alan Ball sat at the bar. After having a good night out, we eventually returned to the hotel only to find our old friend Alan still in the same seat at the bar.

SATURDAY 23 MARCH 1996

After a long lie-in, Coxy and I eventually got up, grabbed our golf clubs and got out on the golf course. I had arranged to meet the landlord of my local pub at a golf course called Toot Hill. Apparently, on a Saturday you had to be signed in by a member so he had spoken to his mate, the owner's son, to see if we could slip in without his dad knowing. The owner's supposed to be a bit miserable and doesn't allow that kind of thing so when me and Coxy got there we went straight out on the course.

Both Coxy and my mate Dave play off 7 handicaps and I'm off 22 so I knew I was going to have to get quite a few shots off them. Everything was going quite nicely until we got to the 11th, a par five. Dave and Coxy both smashed long drives straight down the middle of the fairway so, as I put my ball down, I was thinking I had to try and hit it as hard as I could. Unfortunately, the plan didn't quite come off. I shanked the ball at near enough right angles and it was heading straight for two players on the green 150 yards to the right. After shouting "Fore", they both dived for cover and my ball ended up two feet from the hole.

Coxy and Dave were on the floor laughing. The worst thing was that I had to go and get the ball. I don't think the guys I nearly hit were very happy. I couldn't believe my eyes when I got down there - it was only the owner of the course. I tried to break the ice by saying: "Is that a gimme?" That went down like a lead balloon. To make things worse I said they should tee off before I took my second shot but they said I could go first. I was under all sorts of pressure as they stood there watching. I could feel their eyes burning in the back of my neck as I took my four iron into my back-swing only to tap the ball a grand total of five yards. Needless to say I didn't score on that hole. Dave beat Coxy on the last. They played some really good golf while I kept them entertained.

Went to Dave's pub, the Royal Oak, in the evening and it didn't take long for the story to come out. John Moncur drinks there and he brought along Nicky Summerbee and Steve Lomax for a drink after they had played for Man City. There was also Jimmy Carter and Ray and Adrian Whitbread who live just down the road. It was like the footballers' football show - some pub team though!

SUNDAY 24 MARCH 1996

Villa beat Leeds 3-0 today in a very one-sided Coca-Cola Cup final. Leeds were very disappointing but Villa have had a very good season and deserved to win something.

MONDAY 25 MARCH 1996

We were due back at training on Teesside at 1.00pm so it was an early rise to get to King's Cross for the 9.30am train to Darlington. The taxi turned up late and it was touch and go whether we made the train. As we rushed up the escalators, our train pulled away. We missed it by 30 seconds. We then realised the next train at

10.00am didn't stop at Darlington so we would have to change at York and our connection wouldn't get into Darlington until 12.50pm. NIGHTMARE! We knew we weren't going to be flavour of the month, especially as six of the other lads had been to Dublin all weekend and they had come back last night.

We decided to ring to let them know. Fortunately, Coxy lost the toss and had to make the phone call. He told Tommy Johnson the train had been delayed and we would be 15 minutes late. Well, it wasn't far from the truth, was it?

We eventually arrived at 1.15pm and got so much stick when we ran out on the pitch for training. Of course as soon as one of us made a mistake, the old clichés came out. "Oh, had a good weekend have we". Luckily enough, John Hendrie had a shocking training session, which took a lot of pressure off us both. He wouldn't mind but he had stayed home all weekend. Cheers Happy!

TUESDAY 26 MARCH 1996

We lost in a really disappointing reserve game tonight. We were beating Man City 1-0 at half-time and looked like we were cruising but, in the second half, we were awful and eventually lost 2-1. Gordon McQueen was fuming - a very frightening sight. He eventually walked out of the dressing room to cool down. I knew it was going to be a bad night when, instead of turning up at Maine Road, we arrived at Witton Albion's ground in Northwich. After looking at the team sheet, Phil Whelan noticed they had a player called Paul Beech, on which he replied: "He should be at home in those goal mouths - they've got so much sand in them".

That was probably the only funny thing about the whole night except when I took £12 off Phil at Shoot Pontoon.

It's bad enough when things don't go your way when you're in the first team. It's soul destroying when you're stuck in the reserves. I don't think I could do this for another season.

WEDNESDAY 27 MARCH 1996

Day off I didn't think we would have. I had a lot to sort out today as I might be moving house. It's something that's probably come at a bad time, but you have to get on with it.

England beat Bulgaria tonight 1-0. I thought it was the best I've seen England play with Teddy Sheringham outstanding in the first half. The second half was a little disappointing. Nick Barmby was not involved in the game, but I'm sure he'll be in the squad for the European Championships and don't forget, he's still only 21.

THURSDAY 28 MARCH 1996

Mike Kelly was back from England duty so it was straight back on the scales this morning. Surprisingly, it wasn't too bad considering the weekend I had - I was quite relieved. I'm sure he must think we have a jolly up while he's away. I trained for three hours and by the end I had legs like Douglas Bader.

Transfer deadline today and there were no big surprises and no changes at our club apart from Paul Wilkinson going on loan to Luton. He's had a really tough year with on-off moves. I hope things work out for him.

FRIDAY 29 MARCH 1996

My 26th birthday today. I feel about 37 after yesterday's session. We trained this morning at Ayresome. What's happening with the weather up here? We started with nice bright sunshine, then in the space of 10 minutes it was snowing, then sunny, then large hailstones. We're nearly in April for God's sake. Branco looked on in disbelief.

We travelled to Leeds in the afternoon and I decided to run a sweep stake for the Grand National tomorrow, £5 for a ticket. The winner gets £90, second £30 and third £15. Juninho and Branco each had a go, even though I'm not sure they knew what it was for. Funnily enough, they drew two of the best horses. Juninho pulled out Young Hustler and Branco got Rough Quest. If they win I might not tell them!

Other players who drew fancied runners were:
The gaffer - Deep Bramble
Neil Cox - Party Politics
John Pickering - Superior Finish

Mind you, as you know, anyone can win it, except hopefully not Viv. We wouldn't hear the last of it.

Contrary to what you might be thinking, reading about my gambling exploits, I'm not Paul Merson but I do like the odd flutter. I never put more than £20 on but I like the idea of it and it makes things much more interesting when you're watching the horses. People do it on the football now and I think as long as you know when to stop and how far to go there's no harm in it.

John Hendrie came into the hotel for dinner late. His wife Linda had just given birth to a baby boy. He was born on the same day as me and virtually the same time. I told him he'll be exactly like me. I couldn't tell by John's reaction if he was pleased or not.

SATURDAY 30 MARCH 1996

A vital win for us today, 1-0 against Leeds. They had been on a bad run and it was very tight. Kav scored the goal from the penalty spot in the first half. It's the first time we had been in front for quite a while. The lads showed a lot of spirit and we held on. They missed a penalty.

We were all quite relieved afterwards. It takes a lot of the tension away. I went past their dressing room and it was the opposite - all doom and gloom.

After the game, we watched the Grand National and everybody was following the race. Just as I thought, one of the Brazilian's horses won and I had to hand over the £90 to Branco. When I gave him the money, he didn't know what it was for - I should have kept it!

MONDAY 1 APRIL 1996

Branco came into training this morning all excited and said: "You, the horses, we want horse racing". He was jumping around like he was a jockey on the back of a horse. He thought it was every day. He wasn't impressed when I told him the Grand National sweepstake was only once a year.

WEDNESDAY 5 APRIL 1996

The Leeds game gave us a real lift and we carried that on with a 3-1 win over Sheffield Wednesday. We played well and really hammered them. This result lifts us clear of all the trouble and we can now concentrate on playing without having to worry about relegation.

It was great for Chris Freestone to get his first goal. He's been banging them in for the reserves and he deserved his chance.

SUNDAY 7 APRIL 1996

Walshy didn't turn up for training today - I don't really know what's going on but he seems to be ill. It's hard on him but it might just give me a chance for tomorrow's game against Spurs. After so long out, I was wondering when I would get another look-in but this has come as a complete surprise. I don't want to get my hopes up because Gary might be alright. I'll know more in the morning.

Jaime Moreno after a hard night out! Jaime dressed up to help Branco get used to the British sense of humour - or at least this is his version.

MONDAY 8 APRIL 1996

After seven months in the wilderness, I'm back. Walshy was ruled out this morning and I found out I was playing when I got to the airport.

It was such a relief to be involved again after what has seemed like an eternity. I was under a lot of pressure before the game because of not playing in the first team for so long. You can play as many reserve games as you like, but it is just not the same as Premiership football. Luckily it went very well for me and I felt I had a very good game. We went 1-0 down late in the second half, which was really disappointing, but Phil Whelan scored two minutes afterwards and we got our deserved draw. I always seem to play well in North London - I wish we could play there every other week.

I felt shattered after the game due to the adrenaline rush and mental fatigue, but I wouldn't change it for the world. I've missed playing so much, especially the atmosphere in the dressing room after a good performance. I made sure I took it all in. You have to enjoy the highs because there are a lot of lows and you never know what's round the corner.

Gary Walsh looks like he might still be too ill for Saturday's game against Wimbledon so this is my big chance to prove I deserve to keep the number one jersey.

THURSDAY 11 APRIL 1996

Walshy didn't train today, so it definitely looks as if I'm playing on Saturday. It's so much better when you're involved. I feel more a part of everything and my training is for a purpose. It's a long time since I felt like that. All the time I was out of the team I did train hard just as if I was playing at the weekend. But when you go week after week not playing and there seems no light at the end of the tunnel, you do start thinking that you're never going to play again and wondering what's the point. It's been very hard.

FRIDAY 12 APRIL 1996

The pitch at Ayresome Park has become very hard recently due to the lack of rain so the club has had to reconnect the water supply to the sprinkler system. It has cost them £300 and was eventually connected yesterday afternoon. Unfortunately, overnight we had very heavy rain so the pitch ended up like a bog after being watered all yesterday afternoon. Sod's Law!

SATURDAY 13 APRIL 1996

A really poor game and result for us today. Wimbledon beat us 2-1 and the less said the better, I think. The gaffer summed it up when he said he was bored. I knew we were in trouble when Branco gave us a team talk while we were waiting for the manager. It was as follows, in broken English:

"Today Wimbledon very difficult, long ball, long ball, us we pass, pass, pass, pass, pass, pass, pass, cross Goal, 1-0, Yarm 85, lager, beer, Macky Millers."

I think he meant Macmillan's Night-club.

SUNDAY 14 APRIL 1996

After Manchester United lost 3-1 yesterday, Newcastle took advantage when they beat Villa 1-0 today. I think this is great because hopefully it will go to the wire and that will make our last game against United a real cliff-hanger.

Watched the US Masters with Neil Cox. Nick Faldo was six shots behind Greg Norman, so I asked Coxy what odds he would give me for Faldo to win. He confidently gave me 20-1, on which I bet £10.

After Greg Norman went into the water for a second time on a par three and Faldo went two shots up he very quietly made his way to bed. Lovely jubbly! Faldo eventually won by five shots.

MONDAY 15 APRIL 1996

Coxy paid up for last night's bet. It was revenge because earlier in the season he wanted to put a bet on a horse and I said I'd take it for him instead. I couldn't believe it when it won and I had to pay up. It left Coxy with no choice but to pay up this time round so I'm £200 better off.

Phil Whelan and myself partnered the gaffer and Viv Anderson on a charity event, "A Question of Football" tonight. We took on ex-Boro players at the Riverside. At the half-way stage we were ahead by 10 points, with Phil answering some great questions. What I didn't realise was that the lad who was helping run the quiz used to play at Ipswich with Phil and was telling him the answers. I thought it was too good to be true. I was starting to think that Phil was quite intelligent! It was just as well because we eventually only won by one point.

TUESDAY 16 APRIL 1996

Entered a golf competition at Romanby. It went really well and everybody seemed to have a good time. Ben Roberts scored 43 Stableford points off 18. I'm sure his handicap will be cut next time. Gordon McQueen won the pairs and was presented with a Romanby Golf Club Cap. After looking inside it for five minutes, he realised there was nothing in there and the cap was the prize. He then said: "How am I going to explain to my wife that I was late in because I had to stay for the awards ceremony and then show her this cap?"

Later in the evening, we went along to attend a benefit do for the former Boro star Bernie Slaven. I was asked to draw the first prize in the raffle. When I announced the number, Phil Whelan cheered and came up with his ticket, knowing full well it wasn't his number. I said over the mike: "What a nice gesture, he's putting the prize back in". Someone in the audience had obviously won it and had the winning ticket but was either confused or too embarrassed to come forward.

I saw my old Boro team-mate, Steve Pears, there. He was talking about maybe retiring at the end of the season. I hope he doesn't. I think he's still got far too much to offer.

WEDNESDAY 17 APRIL 1996

Viv ran all of us ragged today knowing that we've got a few days off coming up. After training we were discussing where to go tomorrow. We're spending the day together to wet John Hendrie's baby's head (not literally). A few of us wanted to go to Ripon Races - myself, Phil, Coxy, Ben, Wilko - the others just wanted to go bowling (yawn!). In the end it was decided to vote on it and it was level so John had the casting vote and he decided to go for the gee-gees!

THURSDAY 18 APRIL 1996

Straight after training we were all on the coach and straight off to Ripon Races via one or two pubs. Some of the Irish lads are not interested whatsoever in the racing, but once they realised there was a bar there, they were quite happy. Funny really, they're probably the only Irish people I know who don't like horse racing.

When we got about two miles from the race course it started raining and unfortunately it was in for the day. After three races none of the lads had won any money and it was still raining. I told them they would have a good day! After the fourth (still no winners), we all ventured to the champagne bar where John bought us champagne to wet the baby's head.

At least the last couple of races produced a few winners for the lads, otherwise I think I would have been in for a rough ride home. We had the obligatory sing-song on the way home started by John Hendrie singing all the wrong words as usual - or was that the effects of the bubbly?

After eating, we all ended up at The Theatre night-club for 70's night. Great music, good laugh. A good day out.

SUNDAY 21 APRIL 1996

It was the last day's training at Ayresome Park today before it all gets auctioned and eventually pulled down for housing. It was a sad day really, especially for people up here who have a lot of very fond memories of the place. But when you see how the club has gone forward in the last year at the Cellnet Riverside Stadium, I'm sure everybody would agree that it was the right decision to leave the famous old ground.

MONDAY 22 APRIL 1996

Trained at Kirklevington Prison today which was a result for those of us who live in Yarm. We're literally two minutes over the road so, after training, we all decided to take our training kit home and have an extra 45 minutes in bed tomorrow morning.

Curtis Fleming and Alan Moore were called up into the Republic of Ireland full squad last week which was brilliant for them. With Nick

Barmby and Derek Whyte also playing for their respective countries, it just shows again how far the club has come. We have got so many internationals away for games and that's not including Juninho and Branco.

THURSDAY 25 APRIL 1996

The gaffer and Viv have both signed new contracts with the club and are now both contracted until 1999. This is great news for the club and it's supporters, especially after all the speculation surrounding the England job. I think Robbo has made the right decision. He obviously wants to make the club really big and I think, with the backing of chairman Steve Gibson, it won't be long before he does that.

FRIDAY 26 APRIL 1996

The gaffer pulled me over before training today and told me he was going to play me against Liverpool tomorrow, but Walshy would play against Manchester United because it would be "nice!" for him. "Is that alright?" he asked. I was just about to say: "No it's not f***ing alright", when, of all people, Walshy walked in right on cue. He then told Gary what he was going to do and we all walked out to train. On the way out he stopped me and said: "We'll talk about it afterwards".

I couldn't believe what I was hearing. I've never heard of any manager saying he's playing a player because it would be "nice" for him. It just doesn't happen - or that's what I thought.

This was also said before we know the result of tomorrow's game, or how I might play. After what I've been through this season - starting the season playing well, getting injured, not playing for seven months including a couple of occasions when I thought I was well worth my place back. Throughout everything, the gaffer stood by Walshy. I always kept myself fit during this time, even though on a couple of occasions I must admit I was close to the edge. When I eventually got my chance again I feel I had a very good game at Spurs and an alright one against Wimbledon. Then to be told I've got one game left! I wouldn't mind, but at the start of the season he said to all of us goalkeepers, including Ben Roberts, that whoever got in the team and did well would stay in. That just doesn't seem to be the case now. It's nothing against Walshy because we get on fine, but I know he would feel the same way if the tables were turned.

Bryan has a job to do, he is the manager and he can never keep everybody happy, but this time I can't understand it.

After training we travelled to Liverpool for tomorrow's game.

SATURDAY 27 APRIL 1996

A fairly good performance from us today though we lost 1-0. In the end, we nearly snatched a 1-1 draw when Neil Cox hit the post late on.

I was really pleased with my own performance and won the Man of the Match on the local radio station. I really enjoyed the game and our fans were magnificent, nearly having the whole end. When I walked off, I just hoped that this wouldn't be my last game for Boro.

It's funny because, on the one hand, I knew I had played well but I still wouldn't be playing against Man United in the last game of the season which could decide the Premiership. What more do I have to do?

FRUSTRATED!!!!!

MONDAY 29 APRIL 1996

We all attended the Cellnet Player of the Year awards at the Cellnet Riverside Stadium tonight. Some looked better in the dinner suits than others. John Hendrie told me a funny story about Phil Stamp. Apparently a few of the younger lads panicked when they realised it was a black tie do so quite a few dinner suits, shirts, ties and so on, were rushed over to the ground for them to wear. Anyway, Stampy was changing into his gear no problem, until he put his dress shirt on. He picked up his cufflinks, looked down at his double cuffs which were past his wrists and said: "I don't believe it, they've stitched me up. They've only sent me two cuff-links!"

We all had a very enjoyable night, thanks to Cellnet (free bar).

The awards were as follows:

Player of the Year   -   Steve Vickers

Goal of the Season   -   Jan-Aage Fjortoft

Save or Best Tackle of the Season -   Gary Walsh - something I was totally in agreement with. I don't think there was a better save all season than the one he made against Southampton.

Best Celebration of Goal   -   Neil Cox.
My old mucker won this for his celebration against West Ham for which he appeared on the TV programme "They Think It's All Over".

TUESDAY 30 APRIL 1996

I saw Malcolm Allison out tonight. He was in great form again. He told me a great quote: "The most important thing in life is settling down, but you've got to settle up first!" Nice one, Mal.

THURSDAY 2 MAY 1996

Trained at Kirklevington and everybody looked really sharp. The gaffer really encouraged us because he definitely wants us to play well and beat Man United even though he still has so many happy memories of the place. He told us all after training to rest up and prepare for Sunday's game. I only wish that included me!

Newcastle drew 1-1 with Forest tonight after going 1-0 in front. That now means Man United only need a draw against us to win the title. The only way Newcastle can win is if we beat United and they beat Spurs. I'm glad it's gone to the last game but I wish they both had to win their last games. I think Man United have a big advantage.

FRIDAY 3 MAY 1996

Trained at Billingham Town today and everybody was in good spirits. I'm not sure if it's because of the big match coming up or because it's near the end of the season. Probably both.

SATURDAY 4 MAY 1996

Back at Ayresome Park again today, to our surprise. I thought we had definitely seen the last of the old place. A lot of the stadium has been auctioned off, including most of the seats. When you see the famous old ground stripped of everything, it's then you realise that the club would have gone nowhere if it hadn't moved. I think chairman Steve Gibson was the saviour, he realised that you couldn't move forward if you just redeveloped the old Ayresome Park.

We had a five-a-side match today and I suggested to the gaffer that we should have a North v South match. He then replied: "Is that northern hemisphere v southern hemisphere?" After looking at our players, that's fair comment.

SUNDAY 5 MAY 1996

United are champions after beating us 3-0 and I think they fully deserve it. They have won 18 of their last 21 games which is incredible. People will say that Newcastle threw it away but I think that at the end of the day whoever gets the most points after 38 games deserves to win it - and United do. Having said that, I think Liverpool will beat them in the FA Cup, 2-1. We'll see. Credit to Newcastle who played some great football and I think they were the best team we played away from home this season.

Pointing a few things out to Robbo! I was back in action for the first team until the Manchester United game - one of the lowest points of the season.

It was a nightmare for me today. The less said the better, I suppose, but, judging by other people's reaction to what the gaffer did, I know I'm not wrong. I feel really bitter about it but I don't want to leave so I suppose I've just got to put it behind me.

I felt down but my family was up and I managed to forget about it this evening as it was my Dad's 60th birthday celebrations. We went to the Purple Onion restaurant and they made him a big birthday cake. To look at his face and see how happy he was it really cheered me up. It was his night and I could put today behind me.

A night out with Coxy and Nigel.
Helping out with the raffle at a Supporters Club do.

A Miller's Tale

SUMMARY OF THE SEASON

From a personal point of view, it has been a strange season. It all started very well with a place in the team despite the arrival of another keeper. The team was doing well and everything looked good.

It was then that I got injured. At the time I feared it could mean losing my place but I never realised how long I would miss out for. It was one of the most frustrating periods of my career and I found it particularly hard when the team went on such a bad run.

Just when I was at my lowest, things changed incredibly quickly and I was back in. It was like a breath of fresh air and I was looking forward to finishing the season. Sadly the season finished on a sour note when I was left out for the United game but I can't afford to bear a grudge and I've got a lot to look forward to next season.

For the club, it was a new beginning. We've got a fantastic new stadium and it's packed every week with superb supporters. We've made some huge signings - Barmby, Juninho, Branco - none of which you would have expected 12 months ago.

We started the season like a train and at one point looked a good bet for Europe, but then we had a very disappointing second half to the season. It's amazing when you think that we went to Everton on Boxing Day knowing that if we won we would go second in the league. From that, we went to being worried about relegation in March.

It was definitely a season of two halves. The most important thing this season was to establish ourselves, stay in the Premiership and build on that, which we have done, but after the way we started it seems a little disappointing.

If our season was like a school report I think it would say: Started the year very promisingly but faded away as it went on. A satisfactory year, but could do better, especially next year!

Roll on Season 1996/97.

THE FINAL TWIST IN THE TALE

As I said somewhere in this diary - things change very quickly in football. One minute you can be in the team, winning matches and feeling good and then the next ...

When the 1996/7 season kicked off it was like a fresh start. Last season had been difficult being in the reserves for so long and I was annoyed about the Man United game but you can't afford to dwell on these things. Each season can be very different and this one I was just keen to win a first team place and hold on to it.

The season started with a real buzz. The signings of Nick Barmby and Juninho had been an amazing boost for the club but Fabrizio Ravanelli was in a different league. He was a player who had just won the European Cup and was a regular in one of the world's best international sides. If anyone had said even a year ago that someone like that would join Middlesbrough then they would have been laughed at. As soon as he came in there was an aura about him and you knew he was special. And when he got off to an amazing start with a hat-trick on his debut, the atmosphere in the club was incredible.

The club had also signed Emerson from Porto for £4 million. He wasn't quite as high profile as Ravanelli but, having seen him play, I think he has to be one of the best buys ever. He is a complete player.

When I came back after the summer, it was always going to be interesting to see who the gaffer picked to go in goal. I had started last season but Gary had played most of the year and had been given the chance to show what he could do. I had come back in at the end but this was the first time it was really a straight fight. I was delighted when I got the number one shirt and, at the time, I honestly thought this was going to be the best season yet.

The results started really well and everyone was talking about Middlesbrough again. We were scoring goals and had some fantastic wins against West Ham (4-1) and Coventry (4-0).

When we came to playing Arsenal at the end of September everything was looking good. Suddenly, however, the results started going against us. We suffered some really bad defeats against my old club (0-2) and then Southampton (0-4) and Spurs (0-3). People were starting to talk about the defence and we were coming in for some stick. It was the same defence that had done well at the start of last season but we were being blamed.

I looked at the goals and, apart from maybe two, I didn't have a chance. Some others made mistakes but as I was the goalkeeper I was criticised. You have to defend from the front and it is not fair to blame just the keeper or the defence if goals are going in. There was a free kick from Teddy Sheringham in the Spurs game which I didn't pick up quickly enough and it went in. I hold my hands up to that one but I didn't think I deserved to be dropped. I felt I was shouldering more than my fair share of the blame for something that was going wrong with the team.

After the Spurs game everybody was really down. At the time I thought we had to start showing character and work hard. I was prepared to do my bit but I sensed something was wrong as we prepared for the Coca-Cola Cup game with Huddersfield in October.

The gaffer wanted to see me the day before. I realised something was going on and I thought I might be dropped. I was really upset as I felt I was being made into a scapegoat. It seemed a bit harsh and I was winding myself up all day wondering what I could say. I felt that if I was going to be dropped then it threw my future at the club into doubt. I couldn't face another season in the reserves. I contemplated putting in a transfer request there and then if he did tell me but, unfortunately, he had to go to a meeting and I didn't get to see him.

We trained on the morning of the match with Mike Kelly and joined up with the team as usual. I didn't know whether I was going to play or not and then John Pickering told me the manager wanted to see me. I went in there and he said it was a football decision and he was playing Gary.

He went on to say that with three keepers at the club, including Ben Roberts who he was going to put on the bench for the game, it was going to be hard for me. We talked about it and it was decided that I should go on the transfer list. Within two or three minutes I had gone from being in the team, to being dropped, to not being on the bench, to being on the transfer list.

I felt devastated. I thought the timing was bad and I was really shocked. I came out very disappointed. When I went to tell the lads they were really surprised. A lot of people say there is no loyalty in football anymore but I stuck it out when things weren't going right last season and I think my attitude has been good. I love the club and I was so disappointed that it had come to that. To be fair to Bryan he knew that I wouldn't be happy about being dropped and was prepared to let me go. I don't hold any grudges, I'm just disappointed about the way it happened and that I had to leave a club I loved.

A lot of things were going through my head straight away. My whole life had changed in two minutes and the decision meant a big upheaval for me. I had to think about moving to a new area, a new team, new people. I just hoped that something would happen quickly so I can play regularly. I'll always have fond memories of my time at Boro and look forward to coming back. It's the end of one period of my career but I'm determined to bounce back and, without being bitter, prove a few people wrong.

The best is still to come.